"Sam Logan's *The Good Name* begins with [obscured] sion of personal wrongdoing that makes [obscured] ment to the subject of the book: the importan[obscured] of truth-telling to meet Christ's standards and accomplish his purposes. The book unfolds biblical principles and Confessional statements that should bring most of us to repentance for the unthinking, uncharitable and unrighteous labels we put on others' (and our own) activities, and it also prepares us to deal 'Christianly' with the hot-button issues of our times. This book is exceedingly contemporary, exceedingly challenging, and intentionally healing for the advancement of Christ's cause."

> **Bryan Chapell,** President Emeritus of Covenant Theological Seminary; senior pastor of Grace Presbyterian Church (PCA), Peoria, IL; council member, The Gospel Coalition

"Dr. Sam Logan writes, 'Biblical truth-telling takes work.' After absorbing his in-depth understanding of what is required and forbidden by the ninth commandment, I felt like Job: 'I put my hand over my mouth. I spoke once, but I have no answer—twice, but I will say no more' (Job 40:4–5). His final chapters, however, contain practical advice as to how we can talk about issues on which professing Christians disagree. In this age of the internet and the anonymity of social media, Dr. Logan's wise counsel will move us toward 'speaking the truth in love' (Ephesians 4:15)."

> **Will Barker,** Former President of Covenant Theological Seminary; former Vice President for Academic Affairs at Westminster Theological Seminary (PA); former Moderator of the PCA General Assembly

"Sam Logan has written a book that everyone needs to read, especially during such fractious times. His careful analysis of the ninth commandment is a helpful corrective to the tendency to damage the reputation of others. Shakespeare poignantly reminded us that, 'He that filches from me my good name robs me of that which not enriches him and makes me poor indeed.' We too often tend to belittle or demonize those with whom we disagree, caring too little about the damage that may occur although we are incensed when the victim. Becoming more observant of this commandment could benefit us immensely."

> **Luder G. Whitlock, Jr.,** Served the president of Reformed Theological Seminary in Orlando for 23 years; former executive director of *The New Geneva Study Bible* and *The Spirit of the Reformation Study Bible*; executive director, CNL Charitable Foundation; author of *Divided We Fall*

"I am so grateful for Dr. Logan's clarion call to Christians to manifest the grace and truth that our Lord embodies. In our twisted world, it is sadly the case that grace without accountability can become complicity, while cries for truth can be used to condemn with an angry heart. *The Good Name* delineates the discipline of 'speech made ready by preparation' that we, as Christians, are called to practice."

Diane Langberg, Founder and Director of a counseling practice in Jenkintown, PA; coleader of the Global Trauma Recovery Institute at Biblical Theological Seminary; board member of G.R.A.C.E. (Godly Response to Abuse in a Christian Environment); cochair for American Bible Society's Trauma Advisory Council; author of many books, including *Counseling Survivors of Sexual Abuse*, *On the Threshold of Hope*, *In Our Lives First: Meditations for Counselors*, and *Suffering the Heart of God: How Trauma Destroys and Christ Restores*

"Words matter. Not just the words—but when to speak them, when to remain silent, where to speak them, how to speak them. In a masterpiece written for the layman as well as the trained theologian, Sam Logan provides excellent teaching and insight into the ninth commandment. Dr. Logan treats the observation of this commandment with great intellectual care, but also with a Christ-like attitude and spirit. The Church has a responsibility and an opportunity to be different in an increasingly hate-filled and polarized culture. Sam makes this all very practical as he applies his thinking to specific biblically complex subjects of our day. In a time when it is so easy to shade the truth and bear false witness, this book calls us back to obedience to a key commandment of our great God!"

Bob Doll, Chief Equity Strategist, Nuveen Asset Management; board member: Alliance of Confessing Evangelicals, Word of Life Fellowship, New Canaan Society, Kingdom Advisors, National Christian Foundation, The Lausanne Movement, The New York City Leadership Center, Cairn University, the Wharton Graduate Executive Board, and the Princeton HealthCare System

"Please, if you use words, and you desire your words to comport with God's words, or you are tempted to use labels or you engage in debate on social media, hear Dr. Logan's plea. But, be prepared to be challenged with winsome, biblical clarity to process more, to question yourself and others more—in short, to do the hard work of carefully and consistently promoting the honor of Christ in both how and what you communicate. The church will be grateful for this timely contribution of a scholar-pastor who humbly shepherds our souls to mirror the glory of God in our esteem of the good name of our neighbor."

Mike Sharrett, Interim Pastor, Wallace Memorial Presbyterian Church (PCA), College Park, MD; former member of the board of trustees at Westminster Theological Seminary

"In many circles today, the court of public opinion has usurped the courts of truth and justice. Consequently, almost anyone can broadcast a false report that maligns a reputation, derails a career, and destroys a community. The results are often tragic as true victims are overlooked and true innocence and real repentance are disregarded. If there ever was a time for a renewal of truth-telling and ninth commandment practices, that time is now. Sam has done a remarkable job addressing this urgent need."

Scott Sauls, Pastor of Christ Presbyterian Church in Nashville, TN; author of several books, including *Jesus Outside the Lines* and *Irresistible Faith*

"Some books are hard to read because of the complexity of their content. In *The Good Name*, Sam Logan gives us a book which is hard to read both because of the personal nature of the subject and the call that it makes of every Christian to examine the nature of our words as witness. A brutally honest study in truth-telling brings biblical, theological, personal, and practical insight in a volume that is both compelling and challenging. This is a book that could only be written by one who has faced that challenge and in humility records its impact. This is a book to be read slowly and prayerfully with tears and the expectation of blessing!"

Rob Norris, Teaching Pastor at Fourth Presbyterian Church (EPC, Bethesda, MD); Chairman of the Board of Directors, The World Reformed Fellowship

"Sam Logan has written a beautiful story of redemption. His story is born in pain. The experience of being terminated as the president of his alma mater, after having served that great institution for twenty-seven years as distinguished professor and president could have left him a bitter and wounded man. To the contrary, his experience set him on a healing journey of profound reflection and careful study of one of the greatest challenges to civility in church and society. *The Good Name* is a great book. In characteristic Logan fashion, his book represents wisdom drawn from meticulous study of theology, linguistics, social psychology and the great creeds of the church. The richness of it issues forth in an eminently useful guide to dealing honestly with the inevitably of conflict in a way that is civil and conciliatory. *The Good Name* will guide us in the affirmation, rather than the defamation, of one another's character and honor. I commend *The Good Name* to you with enthusiasm and with gratitude for the good man who wrote it."

S. Douglas Birdsall, President of the Civilitas Group; honorary chairman, The Lausanne Movement; former president, American Bible Society

"I've known Sam Logan for thirty-five years, and, in spite of his self-confessed struggles in this book (or maybe because of them) he has served the global church as an outstanding exemplar of Christian integrity. In addition, he has been—to me and to many—both a friend and a mentor. In this greatly needed book, he addresses a question, often thought even if not spoken: "Why are so many Christians so very mean?" His reflections in this book are deeply biblical, richly practical, and imminently wise. As we would say in my native Appalachia: 'That's right. He said it. It needed saying!' And he says it with love."

Craig R. Higgins, Founding & Senior Pastor, Trinity Presbyterian Church (PCA); a founding member of the La Jolla Group (an annual mission-oriented pastors' conference); member of the T.F. Torrance Theological Fellowship and the American Scientific Affiliation

"We live in a culture of contempt, where slander and many other sins of speech damage reputations and destroy relationships. *The Good Name* deploys the surprisingly vast resources of the ninth commandment to confront this contemporary crisis in the way we communicate. Drawing on hard-won lessons from his own life and ministry—as well as the teaching of Scripture and traditions of Reformation theology—Dr. Samuel Logan gives practical guidance to help us learn the language of love and unleash the power of our words for good instead of evil."

Philip Ryken, President, Wheaton College; member of the Council of the Alliance of Confessing Evangelicals; author of more than thirty books; former senior pastor of Tenth Presbyterian Church, Philadelphia; former member of the board of trustees, Westminster Theological Seminary

"In his book, *The Good Name*, Logan provides a careful and complete look at how we must live out the ninth commandment. He provides solid biblical grounding, relies upon a range of Confessions of the church, considers historical contexts, and challenges the reader to speak faithfully. Most helpful is his format for approaching the challenging issues of the day. Most compelling is the way he encourages us to speak to each other even in the face of our disagreements. Take this book to heart, and let it speak to you."

Steven R. Timmermans, Executive Director, Christian Reformed Church in North America

"Sam Logan's book, *The Good Name*, is needed in our internet age of rising incivility and increased polarization. Christians often are 'conformed to this world' in reactively expressing their opinions electronically rather than thoughtfully following the Scriptures in general and the implications of the ninth commandment in particular. Logan's book is both self-deprecating and insightful as he applies the Ninth Commandment to himself and our culture of instantaneous communication. The level of our conversations and communications will be improved by our listening to what Sam Logan has to say."

L. Roy Taylor, Stated Clerk, The Presbyterian Church in America; former professor, Reformed Theological Seminary

"I won't say that I'm happy that my friend (and fellow sinner!) Sam Logan once committed the sin of 'shading the truth' in his leadership role. But I will say that I'm happy that the occasion inspired him to write this fine book about what goals and qualities for human community the Lord had in mind when he commanded us not to 'bear false witness.' This book is a marvelous resource of much-needed biblically grounded wisdom for believers who are called to 'live out the truth' in a culture—and even, these days, in our churches!—where the value of words is increasingly under attack."

Richard Mouw, President Emeritus of Fuller Theological Seminary; current Professor of Faith and Public Life at Fuller; former President of the Association of Theological Schools; recipient of the Abraham Kuyper Prize for Excellence in Reformed Theology and Public Life; author of more than twenty books, including *Uncommon Decency: Christian Civility in an Uncivil World*

"In an era when the person who yells the loudest or makes the most outrageous claim is the person who is heard in the public square, in

The Good Name Sam Logan urges followers of Jesus Christ to stop and think before engaging. When Christians speak, whether on social media or in face-to-face conversations, they are also representing their Savior and Lord.

Addressing how to think and speak biblically in this divisive, polarized culture, Logan expounds extensively on the biblical and confessional affirmations that address the 'power of our words,' with a special focus on the ninth commandment. Examples from church history are cited to show where failure to manage well this power led to unnecessary division in the church and a compromised witness for the gospel. A significant contribution is his thinking about honoring 'the good name' of your neighbor, and how to honor this often-overlooked part of the Commandment to not bear false witness.

Out of this exposition comes helpful and (in some cases) challenging guidance for how to speak into current hot topics such as abortion, evolution, women in ministry leadership, social justice and same-sex marriage. While the confessional study draws primarily from Reformed confessions, any Christian committed to biblically-based behavior life in this important area will benefit greatly from *The Good Name*."

Jeff Jeremiah, Stated Clerk of the Evangelical Presbyterian Church (EPC); former senior pastor of First Evangelical Presbyterian Church, Renton, WA

"Dr Logan's analysis of the ninth commandment is a salutary reminder of the importance of a good name, and how easily Christians ignore the teaching of Scripture in bearing false witness, either maliciously or unintentionally. That Dr. Logan's study emanated from his own self-confessed breach of the ninth commandment heightens the awareness of the reader's need tSho reflect upon the use of their own tongue, as it did for me. This study contains theological and historical reflections, but is also full of wise advice as to how we should engage in discourse, especially when discussing controversial issues, so that our speech might always be gracious, protecting others' good name, as we seek to glorify God."

Glenn Davies, Archbishop of Sydney and Metropolitan of the Province of New South Wales in the Anglican Church of Australia; member of the following boards: The Lausanne Committee for World Evangelization, The Global Anglican Relief & Development Board, and The Gafcon Primates Council

THE GOOD NAME

THE POWER OF WORDS
TO HURT OR HEAL

Samuel T. Logan, Jr.

New
Growth
Press
www.newgrowthpress.com

New Growth Press, Greensboro, NC 27404
www.newgrowthpress.com
Copyright ©2019 by Samuel T. Logan, Jr.

All rights reserved. No part of this publication may be reproduced, stored in a retrieval system, or transmitted in any form by any means, electronic, mechanical, photocopy, recording, or otherwise, without the prior permission of the publisher, except as provided by USA copyright law.

Unless otherwise indicated, Scripture quotations are taken from the Holy Bible, New International Version®, NIV®. Copyright © 1973, 1978, 1984, 2011 by Biblica, Inc.® Used by permission. All rights reserved worldwide.

Scripture quotations marked ESV are from the ESV® Bible (The Holy Bible, English Standard Version®), copyright © 2001 by Crossway, a publishing ministry of Good News Publishers. Used by permission. All rights reserved.

Cover Design: faceoutstudio, faceoutstudio.com
Typesetting: Professional Publishing Services, christycallahan.com

ISBN 978-1-64507-028-3 (Print)
ISBN 978-1-64507-035-1 (ebook)

Library of Congress Cataloging-in-Publication Data on file

Printed in the United States of America

27 26 25 24 23 22 21 20 19   1 2 3 4 5

To Susan, Talbot, and Eric
Whom the Lord used to fulfill this promise
described in Psalm 127:3

Sons are a precious heritage,
A blessing from the Lord;
The children that are born to us
Are truly His reward.

Psalm 127, **Sing Psalms**
The Free Church of Scotland, 2002

CONTENTS

ACKNOWLEDGMENTS

If I were to thank everyone who made this book possible, the present section would be as long as the rest of the book. But I really do need to mention a few specific people.

Thank you, Barbara Juliani and the entire staff of New Growth, not only for your willingness to publish this material but also for your patience with me as I wrestled with a wide variety of issues related to its publication.

The book would not exist without the work of several tireless editors—Ruth Castle, Lisa Eary, and Jack Klumpenhower. The three of you made extraordinary contributions to whatever is of value here and you did it in ways that, to paraphrase the title of one of Jack's books, "showed me Jesus."

Then there are those men and women who advised and helped Susan and me through the professional and spiritual trauma which I describe in the "Introduction." Again, there are too many to name but here are a few (listed alphabetically): Bob and Katherine Arthur, John Bettler, Brevard Childs (d.), Sally Cummings (d.), Clair Davis, Erik Davis, Bob Doll, Jim Droge (d.), David Dunbar, Sinclair Ferguson, Doug and Rosemarie Green, Craig Higgins, Pete and Karen Jansson, Herm and Sue Kanis, Mike Kelly, Diane and Ron Langberg, John and Christy Leonard, Carl A. (d.) and Susan (d.) Luthman, Carl R. Luthman, Rich Mouw, Ray and Judy Parnell, Rick (d.) and

Barbara Perrin, Phil Petronis, Matt Ristuccia, Leo Schuster, Andy Selle, Paul Settle (d.), Mike Sharrett, George and Marty Smith, Steve Taylor, Rick and Bethann Tyson, Dale and Marcia Visser, Alan and Cheryl White, and Luder and Mary Lou Whitlock.

And, of course, there are the three whom I have named in the dedication.

What a "cloud of witnesses" the Lord has provided—*may His good name be praised!*

INTRODUCTION

The words were chilling:

> "We would ask Dr. Logan to consider that, though mo-
> tivated by, we believe, the good of Westminster Theo-
> logical Seminary, he has been guilty of shading the
> truth and thus bearing false witness as well as failure
> in wisdom and discernment, and to make appropriate
> confession to offended parties."

This was the official statement of Westminster's board of
trustees in December of 2003. It represented the beginning of
the end of my presidency at that seminary.

Of course, several issues played a role. But the only official
statement from the board about what I had done wrong was
the one cited above: I had violated the ninth commandment by
bearing false witness. I had told a lie in a faculty meeting—one lie.

Some may wonder if that is such a bad thing, so bad that
I deserved to lose my job as president of a seminary. Well, the
board's decision helped start me on a kind of pilgrimage that
has resulted in this book, and the conclusion of this book is
that, yes, it is that bad. My purpose in writing is to show that,
as Christians, our words exist to reflect Christ's character—
his holy concern for God's good name, his constant love for
others, and his absolutely reliable truth. When our words are

scornful, selfish, or false, they dishonor Christ. And especially when we speak such words to or about fellow Christians, they cause great damage in Christ's church. We all must learn to use our words with godly care, I first of all.

Because my story is part of this book, I will briefly mention some background. In 2003, we at Westminster were attempting to expand our ministry beyond our main campus near Philadelphia to another part of the United States. As part of that effort, our board had agreed to provide a certain level of financial support for that new work. A supporter of the new campus also quietly made a financial commitment beyond what the board pledged, promising that he would either raise the additional amount or give it personally.

But when word got back to our main campus, there was significant concern. In the aftermath of the September 11, 2001 attacks, the global economy had slipped into recession and general contributions to the seminary were down. We were struggling to make our budgets, and some individuals in the community were unsure that a financial commitment to the new campus was wise. The matter came up at a faculty meeting, and I was specifically asked how the amount promised in support of the new work came to be increased. I froze and then answered, "I don't know." In the moment, I could not figure out how to answer the question without seeming to put blame on the individual who had promised to give or get the additional funding.

I could have said any number of things. "I need to think about how best to answer that question" would have been the best answer. But I didn't give the best answer. I gave one of the worst answers. True, I was protecting someone else and was concerned about the seminary. But surely I was also trying to protect my own reputation with the board, the faculty, and a key donor. I put that selfish concern for my good name ahead of my concern to honor Christ's good name by telling the truth. So in my heart and with my lips, I sinned.

The board's judgment that I was guilty of shading the truth and bearing false witness was, therefore, correct. They placed me on administrative leave and, during that leave, it became clear that I could not return permanently to the presidency. I offered to transition out of the president's office and that offer was quickly accepted. The board's statement had also cited "failures of wisdom and discernment," but the only specific charge against me was bearing false witness.

Sometime later, the *Philadelphia Inquirer* reported that the Westminster board had "abruptly removed Sam Logan, the seminary's president of 13 years, because he was perceived as too inclusive of liberal or modernist scholars."[1] I was mystified. Although I had tried to help faculty with divergent views talk through their differences, I am a minister in good standing in one of the more theologically conservative denominations served by Westminster, and during my time as president I had hired conservative faculty. Words can be devastating, and *liberal* is not a nice word when discussing scholarship in my theological circles. The board had never said anything like it to me. Had someone else given the local newspaper that take on the situation, and on me?

In the aftermath of all this, I began to think more broadly about the full meaning of the ninth commandment, "You shall not bear false witness against your neighbor" (Exodus 20:16 ESV). Both I and the Westminster community subscribe to the *Westminster Confession of Faith* and catechisms and, as I went back to the *Westminster Larger Catechism*'s teaching about the ninth commandment, I realized that the dimensions of that command go far beyond intentional misstatements of fact.

The word in Exodus 20:16 often translated "witness" has broader meanings. Several modern translations (NIV, NLT, NET) use the word "testimony." And in all of them—because it is in the original Hebrew text of that verse—it is followed by the phrase *against your neighbor*. The fundamental meaning of Exodus 20:16 is interpersonal. It is about how my "witness" or my "testimony" affects another human being. This clearly shapes the way the *Westminster Larger Catechism* and a wide variety of other teachings interpret the full meaning of the commandment.

As I studied that material, I came to realize that I had not just violated the ninth commandment once while president of Westminster, but many times! I had spoken against other Christians, most notably against other evangelical and Reformed seminaries that were our competitors for students and financial support.

And what word had I used? The number of times that I labeled other seminaries as *liberal* (with no nuance whatsoever) is so large as to be uncountable. For example, once when a publication claimed that Westminster was weak in upholding the biblical position on the role of women, my response included an attack, by name, on a sister evangelical and Reformed seminary. I pointed out that they had on their faculty an individual who openly and publicly supported the ordination of women.

My willingness to damage the good name of competing seminaries this way is more than a bit ironic in light of my reaction to the newspaper report about me. I have come to see, to my shame now, that what I often said about others may have been an even greater sin than the lie I told to the faculty. I wanted to bring students and money to Westminster, and I overlooked the *several* ways I was actually bringing dishonor to Christ.

Clearly, I was not living out the biblical truths I will present here. Perhaps others have had similar experiences. Perhaps this little book will help all of us to live according to what Scripture says about bearing *true* witness, so that Jesus is honored as he should be. This is my purpose and my prayer.

I will start, in the first chapter, with what the Bible says about the importance and power of both God's speech and our speech. Chapter 2 will focus on what God's Word says about our words—how we are, and are not, to speak. Chapter 3 will explore how false witness that damages the reputations of our Christian neighbors has had catastrophic results in the life of the church. In chapter 4, I will discuss labels and the challenges presented by social media.

After all of this concern, one might think that expressing disagreement biblically is impossible, and I will address this challenge in chapter 5. I will try to outline in some detail how individuals might talk directly and biblically about several "hot button" issues that currently provoke false witness among Christians who disagree. I hope to outline a general pattern of what it might look like to honor both the good name of my neighbor and the good name of his and my Lord in the midst of disagreement.

The book ends with examples of practical guidelines evangelical Christian groups have recently adopted in their attempts to guide their members and adherents in this matter of bearing true witness. We need to learn from one another as we seek to obey the Word of God.

And speaking of learning from one another, this little book seeks to build upon the excellent work already done by Richard Mouw in the two editions of his *Uncommon Decency: Christian Civility in an Uncivil World.*[2] I have learned a great deal from both his writings and his life, and if this book advances his vision just a bit, I will regard it as a success.

I was found guilty of bearing false witness. I dishonored my Lord when I did so, every time I did so! I continue to struggle with this and with other biblical teachings. But I do desire better to honor the name that is above every name, and I hope and pray that the musings in this little book will, by his grace, move me—and perhaps a few readers—in that direction.

1.

THE POWER OF WORDS, DIVINE AND HUMAN

Why were the words the board of trustees wrote about me so chilling?

Because of what the Bible says about the sin of which I was accused.

Because God's word is truth (John 17:17) and the Son of God is himself the way, the truth, and the life (John 14:6), so any of our words that are not true stand in idolatrous opposition to the very being of God himself.

Indeed, throughout his holy, infallible word, our God places incredible emphasis on the importance of human words. Therefore, "shading the truth and thus bearing false witness" is among the most heinous offenses against our Lord.

My concern in these first two chapters will be to examine in detail why, according to Scripture, it was right for Westminster's board of trustees to take the initial action they did, and why it is wrong for us ever to minimize the significance of what people say. We must not make such spurious claims as to say *but those are just words* or to argue that because speech is "free" we can say whatever we want, whenever we want, and wherever we want, so long as we are seeking what we perceive to be good results. After all, the Westminster board made their decision even though they concluded that I was "motivated by, we believe, the good of Westminster Theological Seminary."

Serious students of Scripture simply must take account of the fact that God, in his written revelation, has even more to say about how we speak to and about one another than he does about our sexual activity or theft or murder. No, frequency alone does not prove importance. But neither should it be ignored, as it so often seems to be in Christian discipleship.

Here is a quick question. First, to preachers who are reading this book: How often have you addressed from the pulpit the Bible's requirements regarding other sins compared to how often you have addressed speech matters? And to those who listen to preachers: How often have you heard from the pulpit the Bible's requirements regarding speech, compared to how often you have heard about other sins? These questions have been given recent and powerful expression by Scott Sauls, Senior Pastor of Christ Presbyterian Church (PCA) in Nashville: "In Scripture, gossip and slander are confronted more fiercely by Jesus and Paul than adultery and stealing. May we flee such 'word sins' by offering words of truth, encouragement, and praise in their place. Words that build up and don't tear down."[1]

My concern in these initial chapters is to provide biblical evidence for correcting any imbalance **that may have existed in our lives and our ministries.**

THE POWER OF GOD'S WORD IN CREATING AND SUSTAINING

To understand the power and importance of our words, we must first appreciate the power of the word of God, in whose image we are created. The Bible has a great deal to say directly about the power of divine language, starting with its very first verses. Genesis 1:3 describes the beginnings of human history with these words: "And God said, 'Let there be light,' and there was light."

The Hebrew word translated "said," *'aw-mar*, contains far more nuances than does our English translation. The Hebrew meaning includes such ideas as "command," "demand," "declare," "publish," "determine," and "require," and that word appears twenty-seven times in the first three chapters of Genesis alone. Obviously, the divine author of Scripture means to affirm a significant creative power in the act of God speaking. When he spoke, something came to be that did not exist before; God's word created reality.

This point cannot be overemphasized. Portions of Christ's church argue vigorously about the precise timing and mechanism of God's actions in Genesis 1. But however we handle those questions, we cannot doubt the sheer power of the creative word of God.

The New Testament makes this same point. At the beginning of the gospel of John, Jesus is called "the Word," or the *logos*: "In the beginning was the Word, and the Word was with God, and the Word was God" (John 1:1). And it was through this incarnate Word that creation occurred: "Through him all things were made; without him nothing was made that has been made" (v. 3).

Of course, the creative power of the words of the Incarnate Word is demonstrated over and over throughout Jesus's ministry in the extraordinary miracles he performs. Whether he is with the blind, the lame, the leprous, the paralyzed, the demon-possessed, the deaf, or even the dead, physical reality is changed when Jesus speaks.

Further, the power of the words and the Word of God does not cease at the end of Genesis 1 or on Good Friday or even at the end of Revelation. The evangelical Christian church rightly understands that God continues to intervene in the world and to sustain it by his powerful word.

Paul says this about the Son of God: "All things have been created through him and for him. He is before all things, and in him all things hold together" (Colossians 1:16–17). And the writer of Hebrews makes a similar point: "The Son is the radiance of God's glory and the exact representation of his being, sustaining all things by his powerful word" (Hebrews 1:3).

In commenting on the Hebrews passage, John Calvin said, "To uphold or to bear here means to preserve or to continue all that is created in its own state; for he intimates that all things would instantly come to nothing, were they not sustained by his power. . . . Literally, it is 'by the word of his power.'"[2]

"In him all things hold together." That which God did in creation, he continues to do through his powerful word, sustaining all that exists. One of the most honest appraisals of what would be the case if there were no sustaining word of power in creation is described by Jean-Paul Sartre in *Nausea*:

> The father of a family might go out for a walk, and, across the street, he'll see something like a red rag, blown towards him by the wind. And when the rag has gotten close to him he'll see that it is a side of rotten meat, grimy with dust, dragging itself along by crawling, skipping, a piece of writhing flesh rolling in the gutter, spasmodically shooting out spurts of blood . . . And a crowd of things will appear for which people will have to find new names, stone eye, great three-cornered arm, toe crutch, spider jaw. And birds will fly around these birch trees and pick at them with their beaks and make them bleed. Sperm will flow slowly, gently, from these wounds, sperm mixed with blood, warm and glassy with little bubbles.[3]

Sartre's point is that all of us take for granted that things will continue to be exactly what they have been and what they now seem to be. But in a world without God, how can we be sure? Sartre argues that we can't, and the result is nausea.

Just how far does this sustaining power actually go? Scripture provides some hints:

> I know that the LORD is great,
>   that our Lord is greater than all gods.
> The LORD does whatever pleases him,
>   in the heavens and on the earth,
>   in the seas and all their depths.
> He makes clouds rise from the ends of the earth;
>   he sends lightning with the rain
>   and brings out the wind from his storehouses.
> (Psalm 135:5–7)

> He himself gives everyone life and breath and everything else. From one man he made all the nations, that they should inhabit the whole earth; and he marked out their appointed times in history and the boundaries of their lands. God did this so that they would seek him and perhaps reach out for him and find him, though he is not far from any one of us. "For in him we live and move and have our being." As some of your own poets have said, "We are his offspring." (Acts 17:25–28)

The two quotations at the end of that passage from Acts are, respectively, from the Cretan poet Epimenides and the Cilician Stoic philosopher Aratus. We may infer from this that Sartre was not the first secular writer to be concerned about whether the world really has continuity. Why does it go on existing as it has existed? However one handles this complex issue, the Bible is clear: the word of God not only creates, it sustains as well.[4]

Further, the sustaining power of God's word is not restricted to the natural world. Over and over again, Scripture shows the power of God's word to sustain the human spirit. God's people are encouraged and strengthened when they hear God's words in Jeremiah 29:11, "'For I know the plans I have for you,' declares the Lord, 'plans to prosper you and not to harm you, plans to give you hope and a future,'" or when they hear Jesus say, "Surely I am with you always, to the very end of the age" (Matthew 28:20). More examples of Bible passages that show how God's word sustains our spirits are in the second appendix to this book.

Many verses of Psalm 119 talk specifically about the sustaining power of God's word in the life of faith:

> Your statutes are my delight;
> they are my counselors (Psalm 119:24).

> My comfort in my suffering is this:
> Your promise preserves my life (v. 50).

> The law from your mouth is more precious to me
> than thousands of pieces of silver and gold (v. 72).

> My soul faints with longing for your salvation,
> but I have put my hope in your word (v. 81).

The Power of God's Word in Judgment and Redemption

God's word not only creates and sustains; it also judges and redeems. This provides a critically important biblical model for us if we are to honor the Lord by our words.

God's word judges sin. It identifies what is wrong and specifies the action required to make it right. When God speaks words of judgment, the status of those he speaks to is defined by those very words. In human terms, when a person is officially judged to be guilty in a court of law, that person has a different standing in the community than was the case before that judgment was rendered. God's words of judgment are surer than those of any human court and potentially have far more lasting (even eternal) effects on those judged.

Just as clearly, God's words of redemption alter the status of the person or persons about whom they are spoken. They are more than hopeful opinion. They are facts in the instant God speaks them. They are absolutely determinative. They accomplish what they describe.

Throughout his ministry, Jesus both judged and redeemed. To those who would not believe, he spoke eternal judgment. "Woe to you, teachers of the law and Pharisees, you hypocrites! You shut the door of the kingdom of heaven in people's faces. You yourselves do not enter, nor will you let those enter who are trying to" (Matthew 23:13).

But to those with faith, Jesus spoke words of redemption, as when some friends brought a paralyzed man to him. "When Jesus saw their faith, he said to the man, 'Take heart, son; your sins are forgiven'" (Matthew 9:2). This pronouncement caused a stir about whether or not Jesus had the authority to use such words. But after Jesus healed the man, the crowd recognized the power of his words: "They were filled with awe; and they praised God, who had given such authority to man" (v. 7).

The most remarkable thing about the Incarnate Word is that, *in himself*, he was both the Word of judgment and the Word of redemption. Indeed, we might even say that in his death he became judgment and in his resurrection he *became* redemption. In that way, by his life and death and resurrection Jesus created the church, the redeemed people of God. As God's word in Genesis created all things, condemned sin, and accomplished redemption, so God's incarnate Word in the New Testament creates a redeemed people by taking away the sins of the world.

Martin Luther captured this in "A Mighty Fortress Is Our God."

> And though this world, with devils filled,
> Should threaten to undo us,
> We will not fear, for God hath willed
> His truth to triumph through us:
> The prince of darkness grim,
> We tremble not for him;
> His rage we can endure,
> For lo! his doom is sure,
> One little word shall fell him.
> That Word above all earthly powers,
> No thanks to them, abideth;
> The Spirit and the gifts are ours
> Through him who with us sideth:
> Let goods and kindred go,
> This mortal life also;
> The body they may kill:
> God's truth abideth still,
> His kingdom is forever.[5]

The fact that Jesus is both the Word of God's judgment and the Word of God's redemption is powerfully summarized in Fleming Rutledge's book, *The Crucifixion: Understanding the Death of Jesus Christ*.

> At the historical time and place of his inhuman and godless crucifixion, all the demonic Powers loose in the world convened in Jerusalem and unleashed their forces upon the incarnate Son of God. Derelict, outcast, and godforsaken, he hung there as a representative of all humanity, and suffered condemnation in place of all humanity, to break the Power of Sin and Death over all humanity. . . .

The power of God to make right what has been wrong is what we see, by faith, in the resurrection of Jesus Christ on the third day. Unless God is the one who raises the dead and calls into existence the things that do not exist, there cannot be serious talk of forgiveness for the worst of the worst—the mass murders, tortures, and serial killings—or even the least of the worst—the quotidian offenses against our common humanity that cause marriages to fail, friendships to end, enterprises to collapse, and silent misery to be the common lot of millions. *"All for sin could not atone; Thou must save, and thou alone."*

This is what is happening on Golgotha. All the manifold biblical images with their richness, complexity, and depth come together as one to say this: the righteousness of God is revealed in the cross of Christ.[6]

HUMAN BEINGS AS THE IMAGE OF GOD

How does the power of God's word lead to the power of human words? Surely, there is a difference between God and human beings. What is true when God speaks is not automatically true when human beings speak. This is extremely important.

For example, in no sense do the words of human beings bring matter into being from nothingness as did God's words in creation. In no sense do the words of any human being cause condemnation or salvation in and of themselves. We must never forget the cosmic gulf between God and human beings.

But also, in no sense may we forget the specific point God makes in Genesis 1:26–27. After creating the light and the dark and the dry land and the waters and the birds of the sky and the fish of the sea and the beasts of the earth, God paused. And then he said, "Let us make mankind in our image, in our likeness, so that they may rule over the fish of the sea and the birds in the sky, over the livestock and all the wild animals, and over all the creatures that move along the ground."

And it was done.

Human beings, male and female, were made in the image of God. Nothing else was.

Therefore, it seems appropriate to consider what exactly this means. J. I. Packer has written, "*Image* means representative likeness—which tells us at once that we should be reflecting, at our creaturely level, what Genesis 1 shows God is and does."[7]

Human beings are certainly not God, but they are like God. That "likeness" takes on a very specific form in Genesis 2:18–20. "The Lord God said, 'It is not good for the man to be alone. I will make a helper suitable for him.' Now the Lord God had formed out of the ground all the wild animals and all the birds in the sky. He brought them to the man to see what he would name them; and whatever the man called each living creature, that was its name. So the man gave names to all the livestock, the birds in the sky and all the wild animals. But for Adam no suitable helper was found."

Often, interpreters focus their comments on this passage on the fact that no animal was a suitable helper for Adam. But as important as that truth may be, we must note carefully the nature of the task that God gave to Adam—the task of naming. Implied in what God directs Adam to do is the creation of language and words. The text does not tell us whether Adam spoke the names audibly, but the giving of names surely implies some sort of language. Before Adam, no creature is said to have been in the image of God and no other creature is given the task of naming. Language itself seems to be an essential aspect of the image of God. And the use of language seems to play an essential role in being human.

However, and of critical importance, we must note that Adam does not instruct God to name things; God instructs Adam. Human beings are the creatures, not the Creator, and we must never forget that distinction. Human beings are in God's image, not the reverse.

Furthermore, sin has marred the image, and that has huge effects on all aspects of humanity, not least on the ways in which we speak. Sinclair Ferguson describes powerfully the effect of the Fall on men and women:

> Theologians have often discussed an interesting question here. Does Scripture teach that man is no longer in the image of God? Or does it suggest that the image remains but has been grossly defaced? In many ways, that is a more tragic prospect. We might well be justified in thinking that there could be no greater disaster than that the likeness of God should be exterminated. But in fact there is. What if the image of God, in which his greatness and glory are reflected, become a distortion of his character? What if, instead of reflecting his glory, man begins to reflect the very antithesis of God? What if God's image becomes an anti-god? This, essentially, is the affront which fallen man is to God.[8]

Our speaking God created a speaking humanity. Both our finitude (the fact that our knowledge is limited in space and time) and our sin (the fact that we are corrupted by our disobedience to God's law) affect our speaking. But neither destroys the basic biblical fact that, in our speaking, we are in some ways imaging our Creator. Therefore, we must be sure that our speaking does not become, as Ferguson puts it, an anti-god. Given the enormous power of words, and the way they connect us to God himself, we must take great care with them and use them for the life-giving purposes God intended.

Again, Scripture is our starting point in understanding what this means.

In both Testaments, human beings often speak words God has specifically given them to speak. In a sense, any part of the

Bible is an example of this, because whatever we have in Scripture came through human beings via God's direct inspiration. But beyond this, there are many examples of how words spoken by human beings can have effects similar (but not identical) to the effects of God's own words.

HUMAN WORDS MAY IMAGE GOD'S CREATIVE AND SUSTAINING WORDS

Both Testaments contain many examples of what human words can accomplish. All them are mere shadows of the divine reality, but still have significant effects. One of the most fascinating occurs in Numbers 20:7–8. "The Lord said to Moses, 'Take the staff, and you and your brother Aaron gather the assembly together. Speak to that rock before their eyes and it will pour out its water. You will bring water out of the rock for the community, so they and their livestock can drink.'"

There is normally no water in rocks. But God authorized Moses to speak words that would create water where there had been none. In this case, Moses disobeyed God and was punished. Nevertheless, what God told Moses affirms that, in specific circumstances, human language can, in a very faint way, image God's creative power.

We see this again in 1 Kings, when "by the word of the Lord" a man of God spoke against an unauthorized altar King Jeroboam had built.

> When King Jeroboam heard what the man of God cried out against the altar at Bethel, he stretched out his hand from the altar and said, "Seize him!" But the hand he stretched out toward the man shriveled up, so that he could not pull it back. Also, the altar was split apart and its ashes poured out according to the sign given by the man of God by the word of the Lord.

> Then the king said to the man of God, "Intercede with the Lord your God and pray for me that my hand may be restored." So the man of God interceded with the Lord, and the king's hand was restored and became as it was before. (1 Kings 13:4–6)

There are hints in this passage of the kind of speaking Jesus did in the miracles he performed. Some have read passages such as these and have made the unfortunate error of assuming *identity* between the power of divine words and the power of human words, and have asserted without qualification that human words create reality.[9] We must remember the differences between God and man, especially in light of our present sinful state and limited understanding. No human words have the same intrinsic power divine words have—a fact some preachers and teachers seem to forget. But to deny completely any similarity between the two is to call into question the fact that man is made in God's image.

As an ordained minister, I have had the privilege of performing a number of marriages. So long as the proper vows are said and the licensing conditions are met, when I say the words *I now pronounce you man and wife* a new status is recognized which was not there before I spoke. We act in a way that confirms the power of those seven words of marital pronouncement. Both church and civil law recognize the new status. My words as a minister might be said to image the creative power of God's words.

The secular world provides examples of the same thing. When the Chairman of the International Olympic Committee pronounces the games open, they are open. When the navy christens a ship, it is named and ready to launch.

But far more significant are the ways human language might be an image of God's *sustaining* power. Even though we do not sustain the existence of creation as God himself does, human words have the power, by God's Spirit, to sustain other human beings spiritually. This surely continues to be one of the most powerful purposes of human language.

Jesus spoke about this power when he read from Isaiah to describe his mission on earth. "The Spirit of the Lord is on me, because he has anointed me to proclaim good news to the poor. He has sent me to proclaim freedom for the prisoners and recovery of sight for the blind, to set the oppressed free, to proclaim the year of the Lord's favor" (Luke 4:18–19).

No human being is anointed just like Jesus. But is it possible that words we speak might be good news to the poor? Are there any ways that what we say to others about Jesus might help them sense the Lord's favor? Yes, and yes! That's part of the joy of being made in God's image. If our words are consistent with biblical teaching, they surely are an image of Jesus's words. And by God's grace, his Spirit may use our words as part of his work to sustain his people.

Indeed, Scripture does not regard this as a happenstance. It can be and it should be intentional. Paul even makes it a command in his first letter to the Thessalonians:

> According to the Lord's word, we tell you that we who are still alive, who are left until the coming of the Lord, will certainly not precede those who have fallen asleep. For the Lord himself will come down from heaven, with a loud command, with the voice of the archangel and with the trumpet call of God, and the dead in Christ will rise first. After that, we who are still alive and are left will be caught up together with them in the clouds to meet the Lord in the air. And so we will be with the Lord forever. *Therefore encourage one another with these words*. (1 Thessalonians 4:15–18, emphasis added)

The condition that our words be consistent with biblical teaching is all-important. If they are not, we will be in danger of becoming anti-god. In the next chapter, I will discuss in detail what makes biblical words. Here, however, let's notice the extraordinary potential of powerful words to sustain and inspire us, in all kinds of contexts.

It might be the words of missionary Jim Elliott, writing in his journal before he was martyred: "He is no fool who gives what he cannot keep to gain that which he cannot lose."[10]

Or it might be Aragorn's battle speech in the movie *The Lord of the Rings: The Return of the King*: "A day may come when the courage of men fails . . . but it is not this day!"[11]

It could be Martin Luther King, Jr. at the Lincoln Memorial: "I have a dream today."

Or Rachel Denhollander, testifying at the trial of a man who sexually molested young gymnasts: "How much is a little girl worth?"[12]

These words grip our spirits. They can motivate, encourage, heal, or strengthen us. Because the speakers of those words are made in God's image, their words have the potential to spiritually and emotionally sustain anyone who hears them.

HUMAN WORDS MAY IMAGE GOD'S JUDGING AND REDEEMING WORDS

Similarly, human words have judging and redeeming power. The first of these categories, judging, frequently causes great concern among both Christians and non-Christians. And often, *but not always*, we are right to be concerned when someone speaks words of judgment, because the speaker's words fail to take account of the fact that the speaker is a finite and sinful being. Almost as often though, we wrongly reject *any* human words of judgment because, to take words from the Old Testament, we all want to do what is right in our own eyes and we don't want anyone else sitting in judgment on us.

Therefore, the ways that human words of judgment may image God's words of judgment demand extra attention. Even if we claim—and really believe—that we are speaking our words of judgment on behalf of God, the way we speak may in fact be anti-god. Equally, failure to speak words of judgment when and how the Bible instructs may be anti-god even if we claim that we are keeping silent out of respect for our neighbor. It takes tremendous wisdom and much prayer to speak the right words of judgment at the right time and in the right way.

First, we must affirm the obvious difference between human beings and our Creator. Bearing God's image does not mean sharing his identity. We are finite beings, and this affects our knowledge as surely as it does any other part of us. Not even the greatest of Christian theologians escaped finitude—not Augustine, not Aquinas, not Luther, not Calvin, not (even!) Edwards. This means that what these and all other theologians spoke was conditioned by the circumstances in which they lived.

Furthermore, even all human *theologians*—past, present, and future—were/are/will be sinners. All have sinned and fall short of the glory of God. Depravity is "total," meaning it affects every part of every human being who ever lived or ever will live. And that includes their words.

Therefore, even the best human theologians can never be regarded as "without error in all that they teach," which is the way in which the Lausanne Covenant and the World Reformed Fellowship affirm the truth of Scripture. This certainly does not render the words of human theologians meaningless or worthless. It does, however, call for theological humility, especially when human words are spoken in a judgmental way.

But words of judgment must sometimes be spoken.

One of the great scourges of modern Christianity is the sexual abuse of children in religious environments. I recently attended a meeting at the New York Center for Children at which this subject received the attention of a wide variety of religious leaders—Protestant, Roman Catholic, Jewish, and Muslim. If ever a subject demanded words of judgment, the sexual abuse of children in churches, synagogues, and mosques is that subject. And thankfully, such words of judgment are being spoken by organizations like GRACE (Godly Response to Abuse in the Christian Environment). Similar words are being spoken by other organizations and individuals as well.[13]

We cannot ignore egregious examples of sin or error. As psychologist Diane Langberg has powerfully demonstrated, remaining silent in the face of sin is actually a form of complicity in that sin.[14] The question is not whether to speak words that image God's words of judgment, but when and how to do so. Not surprisingly, human words of judgment can cause great offense and can, when misused, create unnecessary ruptures within the body of Christ, as we shall see in chapter 3.

But as Langberg argues, there are times when those to whom we are speaking may be guilty of complicity in sin, and action is needed. Then, we must speak necessary words of judgment with a theological humility that befits our identity as finite, sinful human beings.

The same principles apply when we speak redemptive words. Most often in Scripture, divine words of judgment appear in contexts which also include divine words of redemption. In Genesis 3, God curses Adam and Eve after they sin, but those words of judgment are accompanied by the redemptive promise of One who will crush the serpent's head. In Isaiah, the Lord's decree of destruction in chapter 10 is followed by his promise in chapter 11 of a Branch from the stump of Jesse. Throughout the prophetic books of the Old Testament, one usually finds redemptive words wherever there are condemnatory words.

Perhaps that would be a good pattern for human words to image. If we ever find ourselves in situations which call for words of judgment, redemptive words should quickly follow. And we might remember something else as well. There is no great hymn entitled "Amazing Judgment"! For good and biblical reason, we sing and celebrate "Amazing Grace." There is no Scripture passage which records Jesus saying, "By this everyone will know that you are my disciples, if you judge one another."

We judge sin *and* point toward redemption—always both, always together, and if either gets special emphasis, it should be redemption—if we want to be the image of our heavenly Father.

One of the all-too-frequent weaknesses in evangelical Christian words of judgment is illustrated in the book of Jonah. God himself called Jonah to speak words of judgment to the pagan city of Nineveh. For many reasons, Jonah wanted no part of that. He sought to flee as far as possible from such a responsibility.

That in itself—the desire to avoid speaking words of judgment at all—characterizes much of modern evangelicalism, but this is not the weakness on which the book of Jonah finally focuses. Unable to escape his responsibility to speak words of judgment, Jonah relented and preached. To his great disappointment, repentance and forgiveness resulted. And this is when we see most clearly that Jonah's heart and words did not image God's heart and words. He was furious that the Ninevites repented because this meant that God relented of the disaster he had threatened: "But to Jonah this seemed very wrong, and he became angry. He prayed to the LORD, 'Isn't this what I said, LORD, when I was still at home? That is what I tried to forestall by fleeing to Tarshish. I knew that you are a gracious and compassionate God, slow to anger and abounding in love, a God who relents from sending calamity. Now, LORD, take away my life, for it is better for me to die than to live'" (Jonah 4:1–3).

We want to cheer the Lord's understated response to Jonah: "Is it right for you to be angry?" (v. 4). But how much are our hearts like Jonah's when we speak words of judgment? Do our judging words emerge from hearts which, more than anything else, long to see those to whom we are speaking repent and turn to God and receive his richest blessing? Or do we, in fact, hope that those to whom we are speaking get all the judgment from God they deserve?

Our heart attitude makes a world of difference. In chapter 5, I will make specific suggestions about how we should end conversations in which we have used words of judgment but have not seen what we hope for in terms of repentance. Those suggestions emerge directly from the lessons of Jonah. And they apply to both sides in any such conversation.

I have mentioned the ministries of GRACE and Diane Langberg. One of the strengths of both is the extraordinary emphasis they place on care for those who have been traumatized by sexual abuse or some other horror. Dr. Langberg recently spoke powerfully about the need for redemptive words for such victims:

> We are the church. That means we are the body of Jesus Christ and He is our Head. In the physical realm, a body that does not follow its head is a sick body. That is also true in the spiritual realm. We are His people and I believe with all my heart He has called us to go out of ourselves and follow Him into the suffering of this world bearing both His character and His Word. And we do go—we send missionaries and the Scriptures; we provide food, clean water, education and jobs for many. And we should. We have rarely, however, seen trauma as a place of service. If we think carefully about the extensive natural disasters in our time such as earthquakes, hurricanes and tsunamis and combine those victims with the many manmade disasters—the violent inner cities, wars, genocides, trafficking, rapes, and child abuse we would have a staggering number. I believe that if we would stop and look out on suffer-

ing humanity we would begin to realize that trauma is perhaps the greatest mission field of the 21st century.[15]

The counseling words which Langberg urges are not intended to offer redemption from all of the terrible effects of genocides or human trafficking or rape or other sexual abuse. And they surely do not offer the ultimate kind of redemption which faith in Jesus Christ offers. But they do offer the kind of hope Jesus himself identified with the totality of his messianic mission: "The blind receive sight, the lame walk, those who have leprosy are cleansed, the deaf hear, the dead are raised, *and the good news is proclaimed to the poor*" (Matthew 11:5, emphasis added).

The connection between this passage from Matthew's gospel and the challenge from Langberg makes another point about the redemptive power of human words: such power depends significantly on whether and how we live out, or "incarnate" the words we speak. Langberg's words about trauma as a mission field were incarnated in the numerous trips she has made to Rwanda and other such countries, directly ministering to the victims of trauma and training Rwandans to continue that counseling ministry. Jim Elliott's journal words were incarnated in his missionary work among the Huaorani people in Ecuador. Like Jim Elliott, Martin Luther King, Jr., literally gave his life for his dream. We Christians need to live the truth of the old saying, "What you do speaks so loudly that I cannot hear what you are saying."

And, of course, the supreme example of incarnation was Jesus himself. Human words never directly accomplish judgment or redemption. Paul even labels the words of human preachers "foolishness" (1 Corinthians 1:21). But God uses such foolishness to save those who believe. Paul also knows how significant human words are in God's work of salvation: "How, then, can they call on the one they have not believed in? And how can they believe in the one of whom they have not heard? And how can they hear without someone preaching to them?" (Romans 10:14).

Human words, both judgmental and redemptive, are phenomenally important. But precisely because they are so important, they are also potentially dangerous. How dangerous? In a passage all Christians should study, and under the infallible guidance of the Holy Spirit, James tells us:

> When we put bits into the mouths of horses to make them obey us, we can turn the whole animal. Or take ships as an example. Although they are so large and are driven by strong winds, they are steered by a very small rudder wherever the pilot wants to go. Likewise, the tongue is a small part of the body, but it makes great boasts. Consider what a great forest is set on fire by a small spark. The tongue also is a fire, a world of evil among the parts of the body. It corrupts the whole body, sets the whole course of one's life on fire, and is itself set on fire by hell.
>
> All kinds of animals, birds, reptiles and sea creatures are being tamed and have been tamed by mankind, but no human being can tame the tongue. It is a restless evil, full of deadly poison.
>
> With the tongue we praise our Lord and Father, and with it we curse human beings, who have been made in God's likeness. Out of the same mouth come praise and cursing. My brothers and sisters, this should not be. (James 3:3–10)

Precisely because of the power of our words, bearing true witness with those words is phenomenally important. Just how does the totality of Scripture define true and false witness? That is the subject of the next chapter.

2.

TRUE AND FALSE WITNESS

On August 12, 2017, tragedy struck Charlottesville, Virginia. In the midst of demonstrations and counter demonstrations, a thirty-two-year-old Charlottesville resident was struck and killed by a car that intentionally drove into one of the groups gathered there. One of the many articles written about that event appeared in the *New York Times Magazine*, and made this statement:

> Americans are mired in any number of urgent, messy fights at the moment. But chief among them is the often-cynical fight about *how* we fight, and whose strategies are tipping toward violence and extremism. This argument isn't limited to shootings, punches, or firebombs; it encompasses words and beliefs too. There is a rising idea that violence is embedded in everything from our social structures to our speech— that speech itself can *be* a form of violence, one every bit as meaningful as the physical kind.[1]

In the last chapter, I argued that judgment is one of the ways human language may appropriately image God's language.

When unbiblical actions occur or unbiblical words are spoken, Christians should speak words of judgment. The Bible makes this responsibility clear in many places, including in the ministry of Jesus himself. After pronouncing seven woes on the teachers of the law and Pharisees, Jesus concluded by saying to them, "You snakes! You brood of vipers! How will you escape being condemned to hell?" (Matthew 23:33).

But that is Jesus, the eternal and divine Son of God. Should human beings ever use words of judgment like this? The apostle Paul certainly did so when dealing with theological error in the church at Galatia. Paul wrote, "Even if we or an angel from heaven should preach a gospel other than the one we preached to you, let them be under God's curse! As we have already said, so now I say again: If anybody is preaching to you a gospel other than what you accepted, let them be under God's curse!" (Galatians 1:8–9).

But those words were directly and infallibly inspired by the Holy Spirit. Is any biblical guidance provided for non-inspired human beings like me and you? One of the best general guidelines is in another instruction from Paul. He wrote to Timothy, "The Lord's servant must not be quarrelsome but must be kind to everyone, able to teach, not resentful. Opponents must be gently instructed, in the hope that God will grant them repentance leading them to a knowledge of the truth, and that they will come to their senses and escape from the trap of the devil, who has taken them captive to do his will" (2 Timothy 2:24–26).

For any of us who are not directly and infallibly inspired by the Holy Spirit, the words *opponents must be gently instructed* are an excellent starting point. There are two opposite, possible errors when it comes to speaking judgment. The first is undue reticence and the second is graceless harshness.

As we see in many public disputes, speaking words of judgment can become unfair. This often happens because we fail to consider our own fallibility and sinfulness. For all that the

Bible says about speaking corrective truths when sin and error appear, it has even more to say about inappropriate judgment. Here is one of the most direct of those statements, this one made by our Savior himself:

> Do not judge, or you too will be judged. For in the same way you judge others, you will be judged, and with the measure you use, it will be measured to you.
>
> "Why do you look at the speck of sawdust in your brother's eye and pay no attention to the plank in your own eye? How can you say to your brother, "Let me take the speck out of your eye," when all the time there is a plank in your own eye? You hypocrite, first take the plank out of your own eye, and then you will see clearly to remove the speck from your brother's eye." (Matthew 7:3–5)

The problem of inappropriate judgment has plagued the church since its very beginning and the results continue to be devastating. When I publicly judged the actions of other seminaries without considering the sin behind my own criticism, I violated Jesus's teaching. In a sense, my words of judgment might even be considered a form of violence against those sister institutions. We all need to take more care with our words. Thankfully, the Bible provides extensive guidelines on how to speak words of judgment.

THE NINTH COMMANDMENT AND THE CATECHISMS

The starting point for understanding those guidelines must be the ninth commandment, "You shall not give false testimony against your neighbor" (Exodus 20:16). Given the power of words, our moral obligation to confront sin, and all the warnings about inappropriate judgment using words, what exactly does God require and prohibit in the ninth commandment?

Christian churches and denominations have offered many answers to that question. I will cite in full two of the most detailed of those interpretations—those provided in the *Westminster Larger Catechism* and in the *Heidelberg Catechism*. I will also reference catechisms from other Christian traditions and examine some of the specific biblical passages mentioned in these documents.

Why catechisms specifically? They are time-tested, widely-accepted summaries of the Bible's teaching. Often, they are also the official, recognized positions of churches or large groups of Christians, and as such are to some degree considered binding on the members of those groups. Therefore, what these documents say about the ninth commandment expresses the behavioral expectations within those groups.

The Westminster Larger Catechism

Here are two relevant sections on the ninth commandment from a modern English version of the *Westminster Larger Catechism*, which was originally written in England in the seventeenth century and is used as a doctrinal standard by many Presbyterian denominations.[2]

Question 144. What are the duties required in the ninth commanment?

The duties required in the ninth commandment are that we protect and encourage truth between people, that we protect the good name of our neighbour as well as we protect our own. We are to actively demonstrate that we stand for truth. We must speak the truth and only the truth from the heart, sincerely, freely, clearly, in matters of judgment, justice and in all other things: We are to have a benevolent regard of our neighbors; loving, desiring, and rejoicing in their good name; sorrowing for, and caring for them in weaknesses and illnesses; freely acknowledging of their gifts and graces, defending their innocence. We should always be ready to hear a good opinion of our neighbors and be unwilling to receive a bad report about them. Thus we should discourage those who gossip and spread rumors, flatterers and slanderers. We should love and care of our own good reputation; and be prepared to defend it when necessary. We are to keep lawful promises. We are to think about and practice whatever things are true, honest, lovely, and of good report.

Question 145. What are the sins forbidden in the ninth commandment?

The sins forbidden in the ninth commandment are that we must not distort the truth as it relates to the good name of anyone else in relation to ourselves. Especially in anything that involves a public judgement we must avoid giving false evidence, calling false witnesses, knowingly appearing on behalf of or supporting an evil cause. We must not defeat or hide the truth and so lead to unjust judgements. We are not to call evil good, and good evil. We are not to reward wickedness as though it was righteousness, nor cause righteous acts to be punished as if they were wicked. Any forgery, concealing the truth, undue silence in a just cause, and holding our peace when a wicked action requires either a reproof from ourselves, or complaint to others is forbidden. Anything that perverts the course of justice, that leads to a wrong judgment or a failure of justice is forbidden; even speaking the truth at the wrong time, or maliciously to achieve a wrong end, or perverting it to a wrong meaning, or any attempt to twist truth to imply something else is forbidden. Also forbidden are any untruth, lies, slanders, backbiting, personal denigration, tale bearing, whispering, mocking, reviling, thoughtless, harsh, and partial censuring; Any attempt to deliberately misunderstand another's intentions, words, and actions is forbidden. This commandment forbids flattery, boasting and the thinking or speaking too highly—or too meanly—of ourselves or others. To deny the gifts and graces of God is sinful. To exaggerate smaller faults thus hiding, excusing, or extenuating of sins; to discover weaknesses unnecessarily these things are forbidden. The associated sins of raising false rumours, receiving and believing evil reports, refusing to listen to a just defence are forbidden. Harbouring evil suspicions, envying or grieving at the deserved recognition of anyone, and then trying or desiring to damage it, or rejoicing in their disgrace and infamy is forbidden; as is scornful disrespect, breaking lawful promises and ignoring good things well spoken of. We must not practice things that give others a bad name and we must not do anything that encourages others to do such things nor must we hinder them when they are trying to avoid such things.

You do not have to be part of the Presbyterian or Reformed tradition to appreciate the force of this explanation, especially if you take the time to examine in detail the one hundred and five different Scripture passages which the authors of the catechism cited to support their conclusions. Here are just a few of those Bible texts, well worth reading so that we get a sense of the force of the Bible's teaching on this topic.

> Lord, who may dwell in your sacred tent?
>   Who may live on your holy mountain?
> The one whose walk is blameless,
>   who does what is righteous,
>   who speaks the truth from their heart;

Whose tongue utters no slander,
>who does no wrong to a neighbor,
>and casts no slur on others. (Psalm 15:1–3)

An honest witness does not deceive,
>but a false witness pours out lies. (Proverbs 14:5)

A truthful witness saves lives,
>but a false witness is deceitful. (Proverbs 14:25)

A good name is more desirable than great riches;
to be esteemed is better than silver or gold. (Proverbs 22:1)

"Beware of your friends;
>do not trust anyone in your clan.
For every one of them is a deceiver,
>and every friend a slanderer.
Friend deceives friend,
>and no one speaks the truth.
They have taught their tongues to lie;
>they weary themselves with sinning.
You live in the midst of deception;
>in their deceit they refuse to acknowledge me." (Jeremiah 9:4–6)

"These are the things you are to do: Speak the truth to each other, and render true and sound judgment in your courts." (Zechariah 8:16)

Love is patient, love is kind. It does not envy, it does not boast, it is not proud. It does not dishonor others, it is not self-seeking, it is not easily angered, it keeps no record of wrongs. Love does not delight in evil but rejoices with the truth. It always protects, always trusts, always hopes, always perseveres. (1 Corinthians 13:4–7)

Therefore each of you must put off falsehood and speak truthfully to your neighbor, for we are all members of one body. (Ephesians 4:25)

Brothers and sisters, do not slander one another. Anyone who speaks against a brother or sister or judges them speaks against the law and judges it. When you judge the law, you are not keeping it, but sitting in judgment on it. (James 4:11)

The Heidelberg Catechism and Other Catechisms

The *Heidelberg Catechism* was written in Germany in 1563 **and** is the central doctrinal standard of many Reformed denominations. It says this about the ninth commandment:

Question 112. What is required in the ninth commandment?

That I bear false witness against no man, nor falsify any man's words; that I be no backbiter, nor slanderer; that I do not judge, nor join in condemning any man rashly, or unheard; but that I avoid all sorts of lies and deceit, as the proper works of the devil, unless I would bring down upon me the heavy wrath of God; likewise, that in judgment and all other dealings I love the truth, speak it uprightly and confess it; also that I defend and promote, as much as I am able, the honor and good character of my neighbour.[3]

As with the *Westminster Larger Catechism*, careful Scripture citations are provided in support of this interpretation of the ninth commandment. Seventeen Bible passages are cited, and thirteen of those are also passages cited by the *Westminster Larger Catechism*.[4]

Of course, just because two historic Reformed catechisms interpret the ninth commandment similarly does not mean they are correct. However, what these two catechisms affirm is reflected by several others.

For example, the *Baltimore Catechism* of the Roman Catholic Church affirms that, by this commandment, "We are commanded to speak the truth in all things, but especially in what concerns the good name and honor of others." It further stipulates that this commandment "forbids lies, rash judgment, detraction, calumny, and the telling of secrets we are bound to keep," and it argues that a person breaks the commandment when "without sufficient reason, he believes something harmful to another's character" or when "without a good reason, he makes known the hidden faults of another."[5]

The Methodist Episcopal Church says, "The ninth commandment concerns truth and man's good name."[6] And the *Baptist Catechism* deals with the requirements and prohibitions of the ninth commandment this way:

> **Question 82.** What is required in the ninth commandment?
>
> The ninth commandment requireth the maintaining and promoting of truth between man and man, and of our own and our neighbour's good name, especially in witness-bearing (Proverbs 14:5, 25; Zechariah 8:16; 3 John 12).
>
> **Question 83.** What is forbidden in the ninth commandment.
>
> The ninth commandment forbiddeth whatsoever is prejudicial to the truth, or injurious to our own or our neighbour's good name (Leviticus 19:16; 1 Samuel 17:28; Psalm 15:3).[7]

The Orthodox Church's *Catechism of St. Philaret* deals with the issue in a slightly different but similarly powerful way:

Question 597. What is forbidden under the words false witness?

1. False witness in a court of justice; when men bear witness, inform, or complain falsely against any one.

2. False witness out of court, when men slander any one behind his back, or blame him to his face unjustly.

Question 598. But is it allowable to censure others when they are really to blame?

No; the gospel does not allow us to judge *even of the real vices or faults of our neighbors, unless we are called by any special office to do so*, for their punishment or amendment. Judge not, that ye be not judged (Matthew 7:1).

Question 599. Are not such lies allowable as involve no purpose of hurting our neighbor?

No; for they are inconsistent with love and respect for our neighbor, and unworthy of a man, much more of a Christian, who has been created for truth and love.[8]

While the *Catechism of St. Philaret* does not specifically mention the good name of one's neighbor, it does emphasize love and respect for our neighbors and it takes a further step which, if followed, would drastically reduce violations of the ninth commandment. Here again is the response to question 598: "The gospel does not allow us to judge even of the real vices or faults of our neighbors, unless we are called by any special office to do so." In some ways, this catechism puts even more drastic limits on our inclinations to correct those we think are in the wrong. This required level of respect for one's neighbor truly is extraordinary.

RESPECTING THE GOOD NAME OF MY NEIGHBOR

Where did the writers of various catechisms get this idea about respect for the good name of a neighbor, and who is a neighbor?

First, the Hebrew word translated "neighbor" in the ninth commandment, *re'a*, does not necessarily have specific religious denotations. It may mean "friend" or "companion." But throughout the Old Testament, it also seems to have a wide variety of other meanings. It definitely is used to identify a person with whom one is close, and it is occasionally used to suggest a spouse or a lover (Jeremiah 3:1; Hosea 3:1). More often, it is used in the context of general friendship (1 Samuel 30:26), but occasionally there can even be the sense of the *re'a* being an opponent (Exodus 21:18).

With this understanding of what the Bible says about our neighbor, we should not assume that the ninth commandment applies only to what we say about other Christians. While this book primarily addresses our talk about and to other Christians, the Scriptures seem to teach that there must be no difference between this and how we talk about and to those we regard as non-Christians.

WHAT'S IN A NAME?

I have confessed that I likely broke the ninth commandment whenever I publicly criticized another evangelical seminary.

My desire in this book is that we all come to understand the total expectations the Lord God is communicating in that commandment. This requires us to think very carefully what the Scriptures and the various catechisms say about the good names of our neighbors.

The English word *name* appears 798 times in the New International Version of the Bible, and both the Hebrew word most often translated "name" (*sem*) and the Greek word most often translated "name" (*onoma*) carry the strong connotation of "reputation" or "character." The authors of the *Westminster Larger Catechism* and of the Heidelberg Catechism clearly had done their exegesis when they set out to explain the meaning of the ninth commandment.

The same can be said for John Calvin, who began his commentary on the ninth commandment with these words: "God here makes a provision for every man's character and good name, lest any should be undeservedly weighed down by calumnies and false accusations." Calvin continues, "Although God seems only to prescribe that no one, for the purpose of injuring the innocent, should go into court, and publicly testify against him, yet it is plain that the faithful are prohibited from all false accusations, and not only such as are circulated in the streets, but those which are stirred in private houses and secret corners."[9]

Remember how Adam was given the task of naming the animals. Numerous writers, both religious and secular, have commented on the way naming is a fundamental aspect of human identity. One of the most influential secular resources on this subject is Ernst Cassirer's *Language and Myth*, in which he examines "the notion that name and essence bear a necessary and internal relation to each other, that the name does not merely denote but actually is of the essence of its object, that the potency of the real thing is contained in the name."[10] But it is the Jewish scholar Rabbi Andrew Davids who makes the point best from a religious perspective:

God gave human beings the ability and power to name. Just as God separates light from darkness and dry land from water, this biblical text affirms that humans—created in the image of God—may seek to bring order to our chaotic and dynamic world through the process of naming. The power to name can be experienced in our everyday lives; for example, nothing grabs the attention of a misbehaving child more effectively than a parent—the bestower of the child's names—calling him by his first, middle, and last names.

The rabbis caution us, however, to use the power of our voices and our words wisely. We must make certain that we use the divine gift of naming in a moral, appropriate, and thoughtful manner. We must also reject feeling that we are destined to live with and exemplify only the names given to us by others. Our tradition teaches that through our own choices and actions, each of us can name and rename ourselves. By doing so, each of us can bring honor to God, to the bestowers of our names, and to ourselves.[11]

The power of our words—this is precisely what we must remember. Human words never create reality in the sense that God's words do. But they may create impressions or attitudes and those in turn may affect the lives of others. We must carefully consider this, especially when we speak words of judgment.

WHOSE NAME?

Beyond what we owe our neighbors simply out of charity, when we talk about other professing Christians we are communicating something about the *Savior* whose name we and they together bear. This is one of the main reasons why my comments about other theological seminaries were so wrong.

The book of Acts tells the origins of our specific name. It begins in Acts 10, with Peter telling a room full of Gentiles that everyone who believes in Christ receives forgiveness of sins through his name. "While Peter was still speaking these words, the Holy Spirit came on all who heard the message. The circumcised believers who had come with Peter were astonished that the gift of the Holy Spirit had been poured out even on Gentiles (Acts 10:44–45).

As if to emphasize the kingdom importance of those events, Peter repeated the story to Jerusalem Jews who affirmed those conclusions and authorized a mission to Antioch to "spread the word." After a year of teaching, the results were clear and "the disciples were called Christians first at Antioch" (Acts 11:26). No longer *disciples*, but *Christians*.

Scholars have debated the precise meaning of this word and its likely root in the Greek word *christos*, which means "anointed one." But again, it is John Calvin whose suggestions are most relevant to this study. In his commentary on Acts 11:26, Calvin says, "But when [the disciples] began plainly to be called that which they were, the use of the name served greatly to set forth the glory of Christ, because by this means they referred all their religion to Christ alone. This was, therefore, a most excellent worship for the city of Antioch, that Christ brought forth his name thence like a standard, whereby it might be made known to all the world that there were some people whose Captain was Christ, and which did glory in his name.[12]

When we speak as Christians, or speak about Christians, or use that name, it reflects directly on Christ to whom that name points. Let's look again at the third chapter of James: "With the tongue we praise our Lord and Father, and with it we curse human beings, who have been made in God's likeness. Out of the same mouth come praise and cursing. My brothers and sisters, this should not be. Can both fresh water and salt water flow from the same spring? My brothers and sisters, can a fig tree bear olives, or a grapevine bear figs? Neither can a salt spring produce fresh water" (James 3:9–12).

If we see figs on a tree, we know what it says about that tree. The words we use reflect powerfully on our very identity if we call ourselves Christian. If our words are nasty and divisive, those around us are likely to draw conclusions about the one whose name we claim. Also, the words we use about other Christians are heard by non-Christians and, rightly or wrongly, those non-Christians use our words to define Christianity. Given the power of words, this should not surprise us.

WHY ARE CHRISTIANS SO . . . ?

Let's compare what the Bible requires of Christians with what Frank Viola uncovers in his blog post, "Warning: The World Is Watching How We Christians Treat One Another." Viola used Google to identify the most frequent way searchers complete the question, *Why are Christians so . . . ?* Among the top results were the words *mean, hypocritical,* and *judgmental.* There has been some pushback to his method, but there still is enough substance to his argument to make us see the relevance of concern for our neighbors' good names. Here is the essence of his argument:

> It's not uncommon for some Christians to throw verbal assaults at one another on Facebook, blogs, Twitter, and other Internet venues. As a result, the world sees people who profess to follow Jesus—the Prince of Peace—fighting, misrepresenting one another, and even "blocking" one another. . . .

Civil disagreement and even debate, when done in the spirit of Christ, are healthy and helpful.

But when disagreements descend into second-guessing motives, distortions of one another's words, mischaracterizations of one another's views, and personal attacks, then we've moved into the flesh.

The net is that the name of Jesus gets tarnished in no small way.[13]

It should concern us if *mean* and *hypocritical* turn up frequently in that Google request, and if such words as *loving* and *gracious* appear very rarely. There surely is ground for James Davidson Hunter's powerful comment, "If Christians cannot extend grace through faithful presence within the body of believers, they will not be able to extend grace to those outside."[14]

In summary, when we say anything about other professed Christians, the total content of our remarks—both denotation and connotation—gets applied, whether we intend it or not, to him whose name we share. Of course, keeping silent in the face of error or sin is absolutely wrong. No question! But *how* we speak is as important as *that* we speak, because the good name ultimately at stake is the name of Christ.

Here is a quick personal example. In the early stages of writing this book, we in the United States were in the midst of a very contentious political campaign. On one day, I posted on my Facebook page a link to an editorial which simply listed the various things which one of the candidates has, over the years, said publicly about women. One responder to my posting asked how I, as a Christian, could be so "hateful." I immediately posted an apology and said I was just sharing what had been said in public by the candidate in question, and I promised to be more careful in the future. Technically, it may not have been necessary to apologize. After all, I really was just quoting the candidate. But what I posted was interpreted as an action that was inconsistent with the Christ whom I claim to follow. I am slowly learning that I need to take great care not to besmirch his name by the things I say.

BEARING TRUE WITNESS

And this leads to another of the profound teachings of the catechisms about bearing true witness. The Heidelberg Catechism cautions against "condemning anyone rashly" (question 112). The *Westminster Larger Catechism* argues that the ninth commandment forbids "speaking the truth unseasonably", and that the commandment also prohibits speaking the truth "maliciously to a wrong end, or perverting it to a wrong meaning, or in doubtful or equivocal expressions" (question 145). Mere verbal accuracy is not, by itself, adequate.

Here is an example. Pastor X, as part of a sermon on the seventh commandment, spends a significant but appropriate amount of time interpreting that commandment in Exodus through Matthew 5:28, where Jesus says, "I tell you that everyone who looks at a woman lustfully has already committed adultery with her in his heart." The pastor continues his interpretation of the Exodus passage by asserting that, according to Jesus, he and probably every other man in his congregation is an adulterer. One of his opponents in the congregation later tweets that his pastor had just admitted to being an adulterer. That statement is accurate, but it clearly perverts the pastor's words to a wrong meaning.

Yet, there are times when we must speak up. Leviticus 5:1 says, "If anyone sins because they do not speak up when they hear a public charge to testify regarding something they have seen or learned about, they will be held responsible." Proverbs 31:8–9 instructs us, "Speak up for those who cannot speak for themselves, for the rights of all who are destitute. Speak up and judge fairly; defend the rights of the poor and needy."

No question, then: when confronted by what we understand to be sin, we must speak out. The question is, "How?" How do we make sure all the other requirements of the ninth commandment are also followed?

All too often, especially in this age of social media, it seems that many of us have reduced our application of the ninth commandment to just the requirement that we confront what we believe to be wrong about another Christian. But more than the authors of the catechisms discussed the requirement that Christians speak out, they provided scriptural guidelines for how we must do this.

We must speak the truth, but we must do so in ways that also DO the following:

- Protect and promote the good name of our neighbor

- Demonstrate a charitable esteem of our neighbor

- Seek to cover our neighbor's infirmities

- Freely acknowledge our neighbor's gifts and graces

- Actively defend our neighbor's innocence

- Demonstrate a readiness to receive good reports about our neighbor

- Show an unwillingness to receive an evil report about our neighbor

And we must speak the truth, but we must also do so in ways that AVOID the following:

- Prejudicing the truth, and the good name of our neighbors, especially in public forums

- Speaking the truth at the wrong time, or maliciously to achieve a wrong end, or perverting it to a wrong meaning, or any attempt to twist truth to imply something else

• Misconstruing intentions, words, and actions

• Unnecessarily discovering infirmities

• Raising false rumors, receiving and countenancing evil reports, or refusing to consider a just defense

• Neglecting good reports

These are all extraordinary responsibilities!

To take just one example from the list, whatever we say about our neighbor in any form of public discourse must be said in a way that promotes the good name of that neighbor. One general guideline for confronting sin while still avoiding all **six** of the results listed above is to recognize that confronting sin (as sin is defined by Scripture) does not necessarily require publicly accusing a specific person of having committed that sin. In general, the denunciations of sin in the Bible are focused on words or actions but not on specific people. I would even suggest that, most often, where the sins of specific individuals are identified in Scripture it is by no less than the infallible and inerrant inspiration by the Holy Spirit. To be sure, there are situations where we are required by our position or our circumstances publicly to name the sinner. But unless we are *required* to do so, publicly providing the name of someone whom we believe is guilty of committing a sin is not necessary in order to confront that sin.

For example, a statement recently made on the internet about a well-recognized evangelical theologian described his theology as "run amok" and possible "heresy," and the theologian was named. But that does not promote the good name of the theologian and it is not necessary for the perceived error (or possibly even sin) of the theologian to be confronted. Talk about the positions which embody theology "run amok." Show specifically how certain ideas presented by the theologian are erroneous and possibly even heretical. But even if there are genuine problems with the theologian in question, a public accusation is itself a violation of the very faith the writer of the statement seeks to uphold.

Of course, one way to sidestep the guilt that may be involved in making such accusations is to claim that the many catechisms I have quoted are all wrong in what they say the Scriptures require. That is certainly possible, but I have never heard anyone openly say so. On the other hand, I have heard many folks who claim to subscribe to these documents say things like the accusation just mentioned.

Further, even if one seeks to avoid the *how* requirements I have outlined by claiming that the writers of all these catechisms were wrong in their exposition of this part of the Ten Commandments, such an individual would need also to explain why the more than one hundred Scripture passages cited in the documents do not mean what those writers claimed. At the very least, any serious Christian ought to make sure (and demonstrate) that the Bible isn't saying what the catechism authors affirm it is saying before dismissing their exegesis of those passages.

I will here suggest one other way we should be sure before we speak. Certainly, it is right to confront the evil of sexual abuse, and failure to do so allows abuse to continue. But at the same time, an individual I know personally was recently accused of abuse and suffered greatly through the resulting investigations and publicity. After many months, the accuser recanted and apologized. Those who had heard about the initial accusation and shared that information now regret that they shared what they did. They cannot be sure that they have been able to do enough to fully restore the good name of the accused.

False accusations may be relatively rare, but any damage wrongly done to the good name of another person is a violation of the ninth commandment and must be seen as such. At the very least, those who have no firsthand knowledge of a matter should refrain from making public or private statements which assume a person's guilt. If we care about the Bible's teaching, we must be sure we have accurate information when we confront someone about sin or feel a need to disclose the sins of others.

Yes, tell the truth.

Always tell the truth.

But tell the truth in ways that comply with all of requirements and prohibitions mentioned above.

We do not have to choose between standing for the truth and promoting the good name of our neighbor; in fact, we may not do the one without doing the other. To put it another way, even (perhaps especially) when speaking out against what we perceive as sin, we must avoid any speech in which violence is embedded or even suggested.

Easier said than done.

But as Jonathan Edwards points out in his *Treatise on Religious Affections*, "The whole Christian life is compared to a warfare, and fitly so." As he explains this statement further, he identifies clearly and biblically the location of the most intense spiritual battles: "True Christian fortitude consists in strength of mind, through grace, exerted in two things; in ruling and suppressing the evil and unruly passions and affections of the mind; and in steadfastly and freely exerting, and following good affections and dispositions, without being hindered by sinful fear, or the opposition of enemies. But the passions that are restrained and kept under, in the exercise of this Christian strength and fortitude, are those very passions that are vigorously and violently exerted in a false boldness for Christ."[15]

My *most strenuous* spiritual exertion must be focused inward, in ruling and suppressing the evil and unruly passions and affections of my mind. Think about this for a moment. Is Edwards correct? Does the Bible as a whole teach that some of our greatest struggles are against the sin *within* us? Paul certainly seems to think so: "I see another law at work in me, waging war against the law of my mind and making me a prisoner of the law of sin at work within me. What a wretched man I am! Who will rescue me from this body that is subject to death?" (Romans 7:23–24).

We are not downplaying the reality and the power of the external forces arrayed against us when we admit the reality of the lingering sin within.

The point here is really a simple one: even as we speak against the sin and error that we perceive in others, our own sin may play a significant role in how we respond to those others. There can be sin mixed in with our good motives. It is usually when we really do see someone sinning that we end up defaming them—and sinning ourselves. So it takes the utmost prayerful commitment to make sure that our response is as God-honoring as we desire the words and deeds of other people to be.

So yes, of course, it will be hard to stand for the truth *while at the same time* promoting the good name of that rascally neighbor who keeps making those questionable theological statements. It will be hard precisely because my own sinful nature leads me to feel about my mistaken neighbor just as Jonah felt about those heathen Ninevites. But no matter how hard, standing for the truth while at the same time promoting the good name of my neighbor is precisely what Edwards and the authors of the various catechisms—and most importantly of all, Holy Scripture—say is my responsibility.

3.

THE DAMAGE DONE BY
FALSE WITNESS

"You will not certainly die" (Genesis 3:4).

Those words constitute the first recorded example of a violation of the ninth commandment. The serpent's lie got the proverbial false witness ball rolling, and it continues to roll to this day. It has crushed in its path many of the good blessings the church of Jesus Christ has experienced, and negated some of the wonderful opportunities which lay before the church.

This is no exaggeration. I will look quickly at several of the pivotal events in the history of the Lord's people, both in the Bible and beyond, which demonstrate how and why this has happened. While the main reason to obey the ninth commandment is simply that God gave it as a way for us to reflect his glorious nature back to him in worship, awareness of the consequences of disobedience will help us understand its importance.

FALSE WITNESS IN THE BIBLE

Human history began in the Garden of Eden, where the Lord spoke his first (and true) words to his creation: "The LORD God took the man and put him in the Garden of Eden to work it and take care of it. And the Lord God commanded the man, 'You are free to eat from any tree in the garden; but you must not eat from the tree of the knowledge of good and evil, for when you eat from it you will certainly die'" (Genesis 2:15–17). Then, Satan lies by accusing God of bearing false witness:

> Now the serpent was more crafty than any of the wild animals the Lord God had made. He said to the woman, "Did God really say, 'You must not eat from any tree in the garden'?"
>
> The woman said to the serpent, "We may eat fruit from the trees in the garden, but God did say, 'You must not eat fruit from the tree that is in the middle of the garden, and you must not touch it, or you will die.'"
>
> "You will not certainly die," the serpent said to the woman. (Genesis 3:1–4).

There has been so much emphasis on other sins—sexual sins, sins of pride, or selfishness—and yet little has been made of the fact that the actual first sin in the Bible was bearing false witness. The disobedience regarding the fruit in the garden, Cain's murder of his brother, Cain's lying response to God's question, the multiple killings claimed by Lamech, and all other acts of disobedience in human history followed from those first false words of Satan to Eve.

Further, note how Satan's words demean the good name of the Creator himself. Not only does Satan lie by claiming that Eve will not die if she eats the fruit, he claims that God issued his original command because of a selfish desire to maintain his preeminent position in the universe. How crafty was that! This statement contains just enough truth to make it believable. But if ever there was a violation of the ninth commandment which "perverts the truth to a wrong meaning" (*Westminster Larger Catechism* 145), this is it!

In a sense, therefore, it would be entirely appropriate to say that the first false witness led to the pre-flood description that "every inclination of the thoughts of the human heart was only evil all the time" (Genesis 6:5), so that the Lord regretted making human beings and brought horrific judgment.

Over and over in Scripture, false witness causes untold suffering and judgment. After God's marvelous call of Abram to be the father of his nation, Abram lied about Sarai being his wife, and this led Pharaoh to take Sarai into his palace. "The Lord inflicted serious diseases on Pharaoh and his household because of Abram's wife Sarai. So Pharaoh summoned Abram. 'What have you done to me?' he said. 'Why didn't you tell me she was your wife?'" (Genesis 12:17–18). In this case, the suffering was visited both on Abram and Sarai, who were directly involved in false witness, and on the nation whose leader heard the lie and believed it.

The tragic story continues with Abraham's daughter-in-law Rebekah and grandchildren Esau and Jacob. At Rebekah's suggestion, Jacob lied to his father about his identity in order to receive the birthright intended for his firstborn twin Esau. Instead of a generous blessing, Esau received an ominous one:

"You will live by the sword
    and you will serve your brother.
But when you grow restless,
    you will throw his yoke
    from off your neck."

Esau held a grudge against Jacob because of the blessing his father had given him. He said to himself, "The days of mourning for my father are near; then I will kill my brother Jacob" (Genesis 27:40–41).

What has been the result of the lies Rebekah and Jacob told? Some have suggested that it is nothing less than the modern Arab-Israeli conflict.[1] Whether that can be shown or not, much of the remainder of Genesis makes it clear that the false witness Rebekah encouraged her son Jacob to bear affected generations of the descendants of Abraham. One false witness—and centuries of conflict result.

In the New Testament, one of the temptations Jesus faced in the wilderness provides a superb example of what the *Westminster Larger Catechism* calls speaking the truth "maliciously to promote a wrong purpose" or "perverting the truth to a wrong meaning."

> Then the devil took him to the holy city and had him stand on the highest point of the temple. "If you are the Son of God," he said, "throw yourself down. For it is written:
>
> 'He will command his angels concerning you,
>   and they will lift you up in their hands,
> so that you will not strike your foot against a stone.'"
>   Jesus answered him, "It is also written: 'Do not put the Lord your God to the test.'" (Matthew 4:5–7)

It is critically important to note that Satan, in this temptation, quotes Psalm 91 correctly. The Bible really does say what the devil claimed. This account makes the remarkable point that it is even possible to quote the Bible in a false way. Jesus's response to such speaking is clear: "Away from me, Satan!" (v. 10).

While there are examples in the Bible which seem to exonerate those like Rahab who appear to bear false witness (Joshua 2), the basic teaching remains clear: false witness is wrong and may lead to centuries of distress for the people of God. Even more importantly, of course, false witness violates God's direct command to his people. Occasionally, God sovereignly turns a lie into an ultimate victory but such exercise of divine sovereignty does not negate the fundamental nature of the commandment. Who, for example, would ever argue that

Peter's ultimate usefulness to the founding of the early church excused his saying that he never knew Jesus? Surely Peter himself would not. When he realized what he had done, "he went outside and wept bitterly" (Matthew 26:75).

One of the most sobering examples of the possible consequences of bearing false witness within the church appears in Acts 5. A husband and wife, Ananias and Sapphira, pretended to give the full amount from a sale of land to the church. When Peter confronted them, he asked, "What made you think of doing such a thing? You have not lied just to human beings but to God" (Acts 5:4). Both Ananias and Sapphira fell down dead for their lies, and "great fear seized the whole church and all who heard about these events" (v. 11).

So for good reason, when Paul comes to provide behavioral guidelines for the church, he pointedly emphasizes the necessity of speaking the truth: "Therefore, each of you must put off falsehood and speak truthfully to your neighbor, for we are all members of one body. 'In your anger do not sin.' . . . Do not let any unwholesome talk come out of your mouths, but only what is helpful for building others up according to their needs, that it may benefit those who listen" (Ephesians 4:25–26, 29).

Under the inspiration of the Holy Spirit, Paul focuses his attention especially on the unity of the body of believers and on the responsibility of every believer to make certain that his or her speech always builds up that body and does not tear it down. That message is also a central focus of James's letter to the twelve tribes scattered among the nations. His admonition could not be clearer: "Those who consider themselves religious and yet do not keep a tight rein on their tongues deceive themselves, and their religion is worthless" (James 1:26).

But the church did not heed those warnings and, even in the very earliest days of the post-apostolic church, Christians bad-mouthing other Christians became endemic.

FALSE WITNESS IN THE EARLY CHURCH

Ammianus Marcellinus was a historian born about AD 330 in Syrian Antioch. He travelled widely throughout the Roman Empire and was a close associate of such emperors as Julian and Constantius.[2] Ammianus's major work was Res Gestae, and of interest here is a statement in book 22 of that work in which he describes a meeting Emperor Julian called with leaders of the Christian community in AD 362. According to Ammianus, Julian had ordered the reopening of pagan temples but feared the church might oppose him. However, he knew just how to keep Christians from uniting against pagan worship:

> In order to add to the effectiveness of these ordinances, he summoned to the palace the bishops of the Christians, who were of conflicting opinions, and the people, who were also at variance, and politely advised them to lay aside their differences, and each fearlessly and without opposition to observe his own beliefs. On this he took a firm stand, to the end that, as this freedom increased their dissension, he might afterwards have no fear of a united populace, knowing as he did from experience that no wild beasts are such enemies to mankind as are most of the Christians in their deadly hatred of one another.[3]

While Ammianus does not mention what the Christians said about one another that kept them so fiercely divided, it is likely he had in view the fourth century controversy over the teachings of Arius about the nature of Christ. In passages like John 3:16, the Greek word *monogenei* may mean either "only begotten" (as it is translated in the King James Version) or it may simply mean "unique" or "only" as it is translated in the New International Version. Arius and his followers argued that it means "only begotten" and, therefore, Christ had a beginning and was thus inferior to God the Father. Others believed that this position compromised the deity of Christ, and this battle raged for the better part of the century.

Both sides in this critically important debate were generous in their use of words like *heretic*, *plunderers*, *sorcery*, and *treason* when discussing their opponents.[4] Another example from the fourth century is what Socrates Scholasticus (a bitter enemy to Arius and a professed Christian) said about the death of Arius (a fellow professed Christian):

> It was then Saturday, and Arius was expecting to as-
> semble with the church on the day following: but di-
> vine retribution overtook his daring criminalities. For
> going out of the imperial palace, attended by a crowd
> of Eusebian partisans like guards, he paraded proudly
> through the midst of the city, attracting the notice of all
> the people. As he approached the place called Constan-
> tine's Forum, where the column of porphyry is erected,
> a terror arising from the remorse of conscience seized
> Arius . . . so that he almost immediately died. The scene
> of this catastrophe still is shown at Constantinople, as I
> have said, behind the shambles in the colonnade: and by
> persons going by pointing the finger at the place, there
> is a perpetual remembrance preserved of this extraordi-
> nary kind of death.[5]

The views of Arius have been rejected by most branches of the Christian church, and a clear explanation of why those views were unbiblical was absolutely appropriate. But the verbal nastiness which Arius's opponents used about him was certainly one of the reasons for Emperor Julian's conclusions about the nature of Christians themselves.

Why does it matter what one Roman emperor thought of Christians? As Ammianus pointed out, this nastiness of Christians toward one another gave Julian political coverage which allowed him to reintroduce pagan worship in the Roman

Empire, something he had long desired to do and for which he later earned the nickname, "Julian the Apostate." The lesson is clear: how Christians talk about one another can facilitate actions by secular governments that undermine what Christians on both sides of any argument actually desire. How we use our tongues matters.

FALSE WITNESS DURING THE PROTESTANT REFORMATION

This pattern continues in one of the most important events in post-biblical history, the Protestant Reformation of the sixteenth century. In 2017, five-hundredth anniversary celebrations of Martin Luther's ninety-five challenges to the Catholic church took place all over the world. This was because the Reformation refocused the church on some of the most fundamental biblical teachings, including the truth that justification is by faith alone in Christ alone, and that the credit and glory belong to God alone.

But a recent scholar has suggested that some of the fallout from those dramatic events was not positive for Christians. In his 2017 book, *The Benedict Option*, Rod Dreher describes today's decline of Christianity in the West and the recent increase in hostility to traditional values. He offers all kinds of discouraging statistics to make his case, and claims that one underlying reason for this situation is "the collapse of religious unity and religious authority in the Protestant Reformation of the 16th century."[6] Dreher explains that once Luther was no longer within the Roman Catholic fold, his one split became a torrent of splintering. Both Luther and many of his followers quickly becoming even more critical of one another than they had ever been of the Catholic church.

One of the earliest controversies among those who became known as Protestants was over the nature of the Lord's Supper.

Was Christ really present in the elements, or was the Supper just a memorial to Christ's sacrifice? The rhetoric among professing Protestants became intense with Luther, at one point, insisting that Swiss Reformation leader Ulrich Zwingli was a "fanatic."[7] Attempts to resolve these differences culminated in a remarkable colloquy in the German city of Marburg in 1529, but the meeting failed to produce agreement, and any hope of religious unity and fraternity seemed even more unrealistic.[8]

Even more divisive to the Protestant cause was the Peasants' Revolt. Luther's initial concerns about the Catholic church had focused on the preaching and granting of indulgences, which were spiritual benefits given in return for contributions toward the construction of St. Peter's Basilica in Rome. Luther's theological opposition to those financial abuses led some at the bottom of the European economic ladder to hope he would speak against broader conditions such as the wealth of monasteries. Roland Bainton says, "The peasants with good reason felt themselves strongly drawn to Luther."[9]

But many of those peasants were profoundly disappointed when Luther did not support a total social revolution. In response to militant actions by which they demonstrated their disappointment, Luther published *Against the Murderous, Thieving Hordes of Peasants* in 1525. Here is how he begins that treatise:

> In the former book I did not venture to judge the peasants, since they had offered to be set right and to be instructed, and Christ's command, in Matthew 7, says that we are not to judge. But before I look around they go on, and, forgetting their offer, they betake themselves to violence, and rob and rage and act like mad dogs. By this it is easy to see what they had in their false minds, and that the pretences which they made in their twelve articles, under the name of the Gospel, were nothing but lies. It is the devil's work that they are at, and in particular it is the work of the archdevil who rules at

Mühlhausen, and does nothing else than stir up robbery, murder and bloodshed; as Christ says of him in John 8, "He was a murderer from the beginning."

Luther advised secular rulers to punish the peasants, whom he said had become "faithless, perjured, disobedient, rebellious murderers, robbers and blasphemers, whom even heathen rulers have the right and power to punish; nay, it is their duty to punish them, for it is just for this purpose that they bear the sword, and are 'the ministers of God upon him that doeth evil.'"[10]

The rulers acted as Luther advised and, although Luther's words were surely not the sole cause, his harsh words likely contributed to the deaths of as many as a hundred thousand German peasants.[11]

Remembering the power of words, it is no wonder that the splintering of the Protestant cause continued, and it appears likely that false witness contributed to that splintering. In my judgment, the Reformation which began with Martin Luther's *Ninety-Five Theses* was overall a blessing to the church, but its positive impact was significantly undermined by how Protestant Christians talked about one another.

FALSE WITNESS DURING THE ENGLISH REFORMATION

When the Protestant Reformation moved to England, the problems continued. In the years immediately following Luther's break with Rome, conflict between Protestants and Roman Catholics (both groups being professed Christians) dominated the headlines: Roman Catholic "heretics" were burned at the stake under the Protestant King Henry VIII and Queen Elizabeth, and Protestant "heretics" were burned at the stake under the Roman Catholic Queen Mary.[12]

But as soon as Protestantism gained the ascendency in England, antagonisms tore that movement apart as well. The basic issue was whether the establishment church had gone far enough in reforming the church, and those on both sides were quick to paste *verbal* labels on their opponents. One of the most rancorous of the debates among Protestants was over Elizabeth's 1559 Act of Uniformity, which required specific vestments be worn by ministers whenever they entered the pulpit.

Among the strongest objections to Elizabeth's action was a 1566 tract that labelled supporters of the Act of Uniformity "silly wretches," "superstitious," "heathenish" and "guilty of the pulling down rather than of the building up of the Church of Christ."[13] William Wittingham concluded that "to wear the attire of Roman Catholics was to seem to consent to their 'blasphemies."[14]

Defenders of Elizabeth's position were led by Richard Bancroft, Archbishop of Canterbury, who did not hesitate to label those who criticized the Act of Uniformity as "heretics."[15] Margo Todd said this about Bancroft: "Bancroft comes across as cantankerous at best, at worst a man of 'vitriolic violence,' manipulative, deceptive, and almost gratuitously vicious in his relentless struggle to quash those who found the Elizabethan settlement of religion still wanting."[16] In keeping with our theme, we might simply rephrase this as "vitriolic verbal violence."

And the worst was yet to come for the English church. The Oxford historian Christopher Hill has written a superb book titled *The World Turned Upside Down*, describing the absolute chaos which characterized the English church during the next two generations. By the middle of the seventeenth century, English Protestantism had split into mainline Anglicans, Puritans, Brownists, Baptists, Quakers, Muggletonians, Shakers, Diggers, Levellers, and Ranters—who all claimed to be Protestant Christians and all seemed especially quick to disparage the good names of their Christian neighbors.[17]

In the end, it took an intervention by secular authorities to bring order to the chaos of English society. That intervention occurred in 1660 when Charles II was restored to the throne with the result that the Elizabethan form of Protestantism was re-established by government fiat.[18] To a significant degree then, the behavior and effect we saw in the fourth century with Christians and Emperor Julian was repeated in England in the seventeenth century. How Christians talk about one another matters.

FALSE WITNESS DURING THE GREAT AWAKENING

The Great Awakening, a religious revival of the mid-eighteenth century in the American colonies, was likely the most important spiritual event in the history of what became the United States of America. Historian Alan Heimert has even suggested that without the Great Awakening there might not have been an American Revolution.[19] The second president of the United States, John Adams, seems to confirm this idea when he writes, "The Revolution was effected before the war commenced. The Revolution was in the minds and hearts of the people, a change in their religious sentiments of their duties and obligations."[20]

But as is often the case in great revivals, controversy arose almost immediately. Some ministers responded to reports of joyful and excited conversions with criticism, claiming the Awakening was mindless emotionalism, and objecting to it in published tracts (we might call that practice *Tractbook*, the eighteenth-century equivalent of Facebook). One critic, Charles Chauncey, said the passion displayed by those caught up in the revival put them in "Circumstances of extreme Hazard."

> There is no Wildness, but they are liable to be hurried
> into it; there is no Temptation. but they are expos'd to

be drawn aside by it: Nor has the Devil ever greater Advantage against them, to make a Prey of them, and lead them captive at his Will. And this has often been verified by sad Experience. Who can boast of greater Transports of Affection, than the wildest Enthusiasts? Who have had their Passions excited to a higher Pitch, than those of the ROMISH Communion? Who have been more artful in their Addresses to the Passions, than Popish Priests?[21]

Note the very strong language Chauncy uses to describe what he sees as error on the part of other Christians. The Awakening preachers are like "Popish Priests;" the devil has made a prey of their people. And if this were not enough, the advertisement for Chauncy's tract applies labels from past errors in the church to the Awakening movement, enticing readers with "a preface giving an account of the Antinomians, Familists and Libertines, who infected these churches, above an hundred years ago: very needful for these days; the like spirit, and errors, prevailing now as did then."[22]

Naturally, supporters of the Awakening responded to such objections. One of the most vigorous responses came in a sermon preached by Gilbert Tennent on March 8, 1740, in Nottingham, Pennsylvania. The title of the sermon could not have been clearer, or more offensive—"The Danger of an Unconverted Ministry." Tennent stated that those who, like Chauncy, did not vigorously support the Awakening were in fact unconverted—that is, they were not even Christians. Here is how that hour-long sermon began:

And Jesus, when He came out, saw many people and was moved with compassion toward them, because they were as sheep not having a shepherd.

As a faithful ministry is a great ornament, bless-ing, and comfort, to the church of God (even the feet of such messengers are beautiful), so, on the contrary, an ungodly ministry is a great curse and judgment. These caterpillars labor to devour every green thing.

There is nothing that may more justly call forth our saddest sorrows, and make all our powers and passions mourn in the most doleful accents, the most incessant, insatiable, and deploring agonies, than the melancholy case of such who have no faithful ministry! This truth is set before our minds in a strong light in the words that I have chosen now to insist upon, in which we have an account of our Lord's grief with the causes of it.[23]

Among the many labels Tennent went on to use to describe opponents of the Awakening are *Pharisee, proud, conceited, crafty, stone-blind,* and *stone-dead.* He concluded his diatribe with these words: "Pharisee-teachers will, with the utmost hate, oppose the very work of God's Spirit upon the souls of men, and labor by all means to blacken it, as well as the Instruments, which the Almighty improves to promote the same if it comes near their borders, and interferes with their credit or interest. Thus did the Pharisees deal with our Savior."[24]

What was the result of this name-calling among Christians? The Great Awakening, which had begun in 1734, was essentially dead by 1745. Its leading proponent, Jonathan Edwards, stated clearly what he thought was the reason, addressing the primary errors he believed supporters of the Awakening made. "And here the first thing I would take notice of is censuring professing Christians of good standing in the visible church as unconverted. I need not repeat what I have elsewhere said to show this to be against the plain, frequent, and strict prohibitions of the word of God. *It is the worst disease that has attended this work, most contrary to the spirit and rules of Christianity and of the worst consequences*" (emphasis added).[25]

Note carefully what Edwards does say and what he does not say. He identifies the specific words which he finds to be both unscriptural and destructive. He was writing just two years after Gilbert Tennent's sermon, so it seems Edwards has that sermon in view. But he does not name Tennent and, even more importantly, he does not fix any label on those who may be calling opponents of the Awakening "unconverted." There are many labels he could have used, but he chose simply to address the action and its consequences. The critical importance of what Edwards *refrains from doing* here stands in stark contrast to others.

Edwards's conclusion regarding *the practice* of labeling opponents of the Awakening as "unconverted" sends the same kind of warning we saw in the fourth century in the Roman Empire, in the sixteenth century in Germany, and in the seventeenth century in England:

> Nothing has been gained by this practice. The end that some have aimed at in it has not been obtained, nor is ever like to be. Possibly some have openly censured ministers, and encouraged their people's uneasiness under them, in hopes that the uneasiness would be so general, and so great, that unconverted ministers in general would be cast off, and then things would go on happily. But there is no likelihood of it. The devil indeed has obtained his end. . . . In one place and another, where there was a glorious work of God's Spirit begun, it has in great measure knocked all on the head.[26]

Edwards returns to this subject in his third and final major treatise on the Awakening, *A Treatise Concerning Religious Affections*, which he published in 1746. In part 3, section 8 of his examination of religious affections, Edwards insists that the actions and speech of genuine Christians will and must "promote such a spirit of love, meekness, quietness, forgiveness and mercy, as appeared in Christ."[27]

But as we have noted, silence in the face of sin can be complicity in that sin. There is a place for "language of judgment," and Edwards provides essential guidance in this regard. "But many persons seem to be quite mistaken concerning the nature of Christian fortitude. It is an exceeding diverse thing from the brutal fierceness or the boldness of beasts of prey. . . . Though Christian fortitude appears in withstanding and counteracting enemies without us; yet it much more appears in resisting and suppressing the enemies that are within us; because they are our worst and strongest enemies and have greatest advantage against us."[28]

Edwards concludes with words that speak directly to my own sin: "There is a pretended boldness for Christ that arises from no better principle than pride."[29] This speaks to the way I publicly criticized other evangelical seminaries because, when I think back carefully over my motives in much of that criticism, I realize that I was actually more interested in promoting my seminary and my cause than I was in exalting the honor and the good name of Jesus Christ. Thus, I now realize that I had violated both the general teaching of Scripture and the specific requirements of the ninth commandment when I publicly shared that criticism.

In addition to the impact Tennent's remarks about "unconverted" ministers had on the Awakening, it is likely that those remarks also caused a fracture in the church:

> Simply stated, "The Danger of An Unconverted Ministry" was a main contributor to the first schism in the American Presbyterian Church. Two years after Tennent preached "Danger" in Nottingham, Pennsylvania, the Presbyterian Church split into the Presbytery of New York and the Presbytery of Philadelphia. Was Tennent responsible for this split or were his opponents responsible for the split? And the answer is, "Yes."

Both sides were responsible for this rending of the Body of Christ. Both sides spoke harshly about the other. Neither side lived in full obedience to what the *Westminster Larger Catechism* says are the requirements and the prohibitions of the Ninth Commandment. But no single statement was as damaging to the cause of church unity as Tennent's "Danger" sermon.[30]

But even Edwards, who saw the negative results which words like those in "The Danger of an Unconverted Ministry" can cause, had his own blind spot, and it cost him dearly. Fourteen years after he saw the Great Awakening begin in his church in Northampton, Massachusetts, Jonathan Edwards—one of the greatest preacher-theologians America has seen—was fired by that church. Historian George Marsden has suggested that, in a strange but instructive way, the ninth commandment might have been involved. In his biography of Edwards, Marsden spends an entire chapter detailing all that went wrong with Edwards's pastorate of the Northampton church. Marsden focuses on what has been called "The Bad Book Incident" but which he prefers to call "The Incident of the Young Folk's Bible."

The back story is this: Edwards "learned that a number of young men of his congregation, all aged twenty-one to twenty-nine, had been passing around books on popular medicine and midwifery, quoting from them to each other in a lewd joking manner and using the information in them to taunt young women about their menstruation. To make matters worse, the books had been used for salacious mirth for as much as five years."[31]

This was serious business in mid-eighteenth-century Northampton. One of Edwards's contemporaries, Samuel Hopkins, who was in Northampton during the latter phase of this scandal, reported that "the turning point in Edwards' standing in Northampton came as a result of a tactical error in his initial handling of the crisis."[32] What was that error? Marsden describes it this way:

> Edwards asked "the brethren of the church" to stay after the Sunday service to hear about the matter. They readily assented to choose a number of the leading men of the community to assist the pastor in hearing the case. This was all standard procedure for a matter that had, at least, a semi-public character.
>
> Edwards announced a time when the committee would meet at his house and, in a fateful mistake, read off a list of the people order to report there. The list included some who were accused and some who were witnesses, but Edwards failed to disclose any such distinction. Some of the young people named were from, or related to, prominent families. According to Hopkins, before the townspeople reached their homes some leading citizens were condemning the procedure. By the time the committee met, "the town was suddenly all on a blaze."[33]

The sin, especially the sin of sexual harassment of young women of the congregation, surely had to be confronted. Words of judgment needed to be spoken. But in his handling of the situation, Edwards defamed the good names of those who were called as witnesses by not making clear their role in the situation. In the language of the *Westminster Larger Catechism*, Edwards "perverted the course of justice" by "thoughtless and partial censuring" and he contributed to the "raising of false rumours." By the words he *failed* to speak, failing to identify which individuals were being summoned as suspected parties and which were being summoned merely as witnesses, he violated the ninth commandment.

As Satan violated the ninth commandment even when quoting Scripture, Edwards violated the ninth commandment by what he *did* not say. And it cost him his pulpit. What we say—and what we *don't* say—matters.

FALSE WITNESS IN THE CHURCH TODAY

Sadly, examples of violations of the ninth commandment by Christians abound throughout the nineteenth and the twentieth centuries. Before turning to make some suggestions about how best to live in obedience to the ninth commandment, I would like to provide just a couple of examples from right here in the present. I do this to make clear what probably already is clear: as bad as the talk of professing Christians about other professing Christians was in earlier days, it is, if anything, even worse today.

One of the most influential Christians of the twentieth century was Billy Graham. In its April 2018 issue commemorating the life and contributions of Graham, *Christianity Today* featured a page highlighting the role he played in the founding of that magazine. This is the quotation from Graham which was cited as part of that commemoration: "*Christianity Today* should take the responsibility of leading in love. What so much of our evangelical work has failed to do in fighting and name calling."[34]

The fighting and name calling continues. I won't name the offenders here, but one prominent evangelical Christian website has recently accused well-known pastor John Piper of "deadly heresy" due to some written comments about the doctrine of justification by faith. Another evangelical Christian website says pastor Tim Keller preaches a "false gospel," based on a secular interview he did about one of his books. To repeat a suggestion I made earlier, if there are concerns about the theology of either Piper or Keller, the biblical way of dealing with those concerns involves a thorough discussion of the perceived problems without naming either man.

In an offshoot of the Arian controversy that gave Julian the Apostate the opportunity to restore pagan temples to the Roman Empire, one dispute today revolves around the question of whether Jesus, the Son of God, is "eternally subordinate" to God the Father. Some of those opposing this doctrine are quick to label it a *current heresy*.

The rhetoric surrounding these discussions has become so heated that one evangelical leader, Albert Mohler, has posted a strong plea that the word heresy NOT be used to describe the position of Christians with whom we may disagree on this subject. Mohler's words summarize much that has been said in this chapter:

> Recent charges of violating the Nicene Creed made against respected evangelical theologians like Wayne Grudem and Bruce Ware are not just nonsense—they are precisely the kind of nonsense that undermines orthodoxy and obscures real heresy. Their teachings do not in any way contradict the words of the Nicene Creed, and both theologians eagerly affirm it. I do not share their proposals concerning the eternal submission of the Son to the Father, but I am well aware that nothing they have taught even resembles the heresy of the Arians. To the contrary, both theologians affirm the full scope of orthodox Christianity and have proved themselves faithful teachers of the church. These charges are baseless, reckless, and unworthy of those who have made them.[35]

Note how Mohler characterizes the danger of pinning the label *heretic* on professed evangelical Christians: such accusations "are precisely the kind of nonsense that undermines orthodoxy and obscures real heresy." Such accusations are like claiming that those who did not support the Great Awakening were "unconverted."

Disagree, yes. Dr. Mohler makes it clear that he does disagree with the doctrine of eternal subordination. But he disagrees in a way that does not destroy the very faith he is defending. We need to disagree in ways that uphold the ninth commandment and that protect the good name of the neighbor with whom we disagree. One of the best general discussions of what it means to "disagree agreeably" in a Christian context was a blog post by Scotty Smith, "When Sharp and Serious Disagreements Threaten," posted on October 7, 2018 by The Gospel Coalition.[36] I commend that post to readers who wish to hear the same message from a different voice.

So what specific guidelines might be suggested toward such a goal? Some have been suggested already and in the next chapter, I will focus on the most important of those guidelines.

4.

PRINCIPLES OF BEARING TRUE WITNESS

Having seen what the Bible requires with respect to bearing true witness, I would like to suggest several general principles to assist us in such God-honoring efforts. Of course, these are not the only principles one might follow. Nor are they to be equated with Scripture itself. But they are derived from what I believe Scripture and church history teach.

THE GOOD NAME OF JESUS

The first guideline is both the most general and, by far, the most important. Before we speak, especially before we speak words of judgment, we must first ask ourselves, "Why exactly am I speaking these words?" All too often, when I have spoken words of judgment in the past, my motives have been questionable, to say the least. For example, I now realize that, when I spoke judging words about other evangelical seminaries, too often I was speaking not primarily to bring honor to the good name of Jesus but to bring students and financial contributions to my own seminary.

Even worse have been the times, some very recent, when I have realized that I was criticizing the words and actions of other

Christians not primarily to make certain that Christ was appropriately honored but to communicate that I was more orthodox. or more evangelical, or more Reformed than those I was criticizing. Admittedly, this can be a very fine line. When we stand for the truth, we will be seen as doing just that—standing for the truth. But how we stand for the truth can make all the difference between bearing true witness and bearing false witness.

My point here is to keep first things first. The first thing to remember when we are preparing to speak are Jesus's words in Matthew 6:33, "But seek first his kingdom and his righteousness, and all these things will be given to you as well." Am I really seeking to preserve and to promote the good name of the Savior in what I am about to say? Am I genuinely seeking first his kingdom and not some version of my own kingdom? For me, this makes a huge difference in both when I speak and how I speak.

WORDS AND DEEDS

The second guideline I would like to offer is somewhat more specific. Remembering that God alone has infallible knowledge of the hearts and the spiritual conditions of human beings, our words should never make—or even suggest—absolute judgments about the heart or spiritual condition any individual or group. One of the most egregious and disastrous examples of this kind of judging was Gilbert Tennent's sermon. When Tennent judged that those who opposed the Great Awakening were unconverted, he implicitly presumed to know the spiritual condition of those he was criticizing. That was an error. The result was that the name of Jesus Christ, whose name those other Christians bore, was dishonored and the work of the Holy Spirit in the Awakening was undermined.

What should Tennent have said? What should we say now when confronted with what we perceive to be errors in words or deeds? How should we also seek to avoid the sin of silent complicity in sin and evil? At the very least, we should confront sinful words and deeds but avoid making comments about the spiritual estate of those who spoke or wrote those words or who performed those deeds. As great as the temptation might be to judge the hearts and motives of others, it is a temptation which we must resist.

Now for some purely practical guidelines.

LABELS LIKELY LIE

I love to cut to the chase with those who are clearly (at least in my eyes!) wrong. Because I strongly feel the need to correct error wherever it is found, I tend to quickly apply some kind of horrendous label to my sinning neighbor to make it clear to him and the world how bad and dangerous he is.

We all know how this works and many of us have participated in labeling. So, my first specific guideline about bearing true witness has to do with this subject.

Of course, labels can have a good function: they provide quick (and often important) information about a product or a location or an institution. If I see the label Psychiatrist on a building, I won't hobble in hoping to find someone to treat my broken foot. If I see Poison! on a bottle, I probably won't pour the contents over ice and enjoy it on a hot afternoon.

But applying labels to people—ah, that is much trickier, because every person we have ever met or will meet is both made in the image of God and a sinner. Especially when we add the qualifier professing Christian, there is a level of complexity not found in dealing with a bottle of drain cleaner.

Let me start with a label that doesn't sound as threatening today as it once did. When I was growing up in Mississippi in the 1950s, just about the worst label that could be applied to anyone was communist. To be sure, there were actual, flesh-and-blood communists around. But in my high school, that label was easily used about anyone who, for example, wanted to integrate Mississippi's public schools. If I and my classmates had been able to go "back to the future" to 2018 and visit, for example, the Acton Institute in Michigan, we would have been absolutely convinced that the place was overrun with "communists" because those folks support the racial integration of all of American life. There is no doubt whatsoever that, at least in economic theory, the Acton Institute is as far from communist as it is possible to get. But those of us who arrived from 1950s Mississippi would probably not have been convinced.

No problem here, I suspect. Most readers of this little book probably agree that labeling people communists just because they support the integration of schools would be ridiculous.

But now let's think about a more familiar label, liberal—the word I once used to discredit other seminaries. What in the world does this word actually mean? All I know is that during the first thirty years of my professional life, any person or organization that was "liberal" was bad. And I mean really bad!! Now the force of that particular label has shifted sufficiently so that we often hear it modified before being applied to individuals or organizations, for example, "She is theologically conservative but politically liberal."

I recommend that, with or without modifiers, we abandon the use of the label liberal. Why? Because the label liberal likely lies more than it tells the truth. That is, while it may be somewhat accurate to apply the word to some facets of another person's beliefs and actions, it carries enough connotative weight that it often fails to promote the good name of the person or group to whom it is being applied. And that is a violation of the ninth commandment—because it is a lie.

Equally, but in the opposite direction, the label conservative is so vague as to be of limited value, especially when used by people who see themselves as something other than conservative. Because of the freight which this label and its synonyms bear, and because of the complexity of human beings, it often fails to promote the good name of the person or persons about whom it is being used. Again, applying it is a violation of the ninth commandment—because it is a lie.

The simple but undeniable fact is that it is not necessary to use either the label liberal or the label conservative in order to stand for the truth.

But wait, someone might protest. Didn't Jesus sometimes use labels? Didn't the other writers of Scripture occasionally use labels? Just listen to Jesus words: "Woe to you, teachers of the law and Pharisees, you hypocrites! You shut the door of the kingdom of heaven in people's faces. You yourselves do not enter, nor will you let those enter who are trying to" (Matthew 23:13).

If ever there was a harsh label, hypocrites is it! Or hear these words from Paul: "You foolish Galatians! Who has bewitched you? Before your very eyes Jesus Christ was clearly portrayed as crucified. I would like to learn just one thing from you: Did you receive the Spirit by the works of the law, or by believing what you heard? Are you so foolish?" (Galatians 3:1–3).

Foolish is almost as harsh a label as hypocrites.

The writers of the catechisms I cited in chapter 2 knew their Bibles. They understood the import of Matthew 23 and of Galatians 3. Yet they still argued that our kingdom responsibility includes protecting and promoting the good names of our neighbors. How could they do this? Simply by recognizing that we are not Jesus. We do not have the power to deliver people from their sins. We do not have his infallible knowledge. Neither are we inspired by the Holy Spirit as was the apostle Paul. What we write is neither infallible nor inerrant, and we must not act as though we think it is. Our biblical responsibility is to do what God says we are to do, not to try to do what God himself and his specially inspired servants have done.

So what am I suggesting here? Simple: if we really subscribe to the Scriptures and the catechisms, we will quit using labels to talk about other professing Christians.

This does not mean that we abandon speaking the truth. But it does mean that we will take great care in how we speak the truth. Labels tend to apply imprecise or broad criticism, often well beyond what is deserved, or they unfairly ascribe characteristics to all the members of a group of people. The use of labels is how not to tell the truth.

SOME LABELS TO ELIMINATE

I will now list some labels I believe we should all agree never to use again. Then I encourage readers to suggest other possible labels we should probably ban. Make this an accountability matter.

But, you ask, who is ever going to pay any attention to a list that a few individuals like us create? I admit this whole idea is utter foolishness—but it is foolishness like every sermon I have ever preached! (see 1 Corinthians 1:18–2:5). And it may also be obedience to the ninth commandment.

So here is my preliminary list of labels to be banned. I start with a relative short list, but every item on this list has been taken directly from public comments by self-professed Christians about other self-professed Christians.

Absolutist
Syncretistic
Legalist/legalism
Promoter of cheap grace
Spreader of false doctrines
Preacher of a false gospel
Fascist
Heretic/heretical
Homophobic
Racist
Unbiblical
Unconverted

But wait, you might say. There really are unconverted people. There really are racists. And some people certainly are homophobic. Doesn't the ninth commandment require us to bear true witness about these people? Don't even the authors of the catechisms affirm that God requires us to stand for the truth? Of course. We are required to tell the truth, even when the truth may be painful. However, we are not required to label other professing Christians when telling the truth.

Biblical truth-telling takes work. The use of labels and other shortcuts may save time and may attract more attention. But when God gave the ninth commandment, he was not concerned with saving time and attracting attention. God is concerned about making sure that how we speak, as much as what we say, fully brings honor to the good name of Jesus.

Let me give just one example of a statement which, in my judgment, represents full truth-telling but avoids simple labels and therefore bears true witness. One hot topic in various Christian circles today is what has been called republication. The controversy is over whether the covenant made through Moses at Mount Sinai is simply a "republication" of the original covenant of works God made with Adam or a new expression of God's expectations for his people. The answer has implications for how we view the Ten Commandments and the Old Testament. The 2016 General Assembly of the Orthodox Presbyterian Church received a report on this controversy—and it was ninety-five pages long![1]

When I first received a copy of this report, I thought, Good grief, do we really need to know this much about the matter? However, as I read it, I began to realize that if the controversy were to be addressed in a way that embodied the teachings of the ninth commandment, then it probably did need to take full account of the subtleties of the various issues involved. And that takes a lot of words! Quick, simple labels would have allowed me to get back to my other work more quickly, but they would likely have lied.

Further, the dangers of labeling apply not only when we are talking to or about other individuals. They may especially apply when we are talking to or about groups of people. If I want to avoid violating the ninth commandment, I will avoid making any derogatory comments about Democrats or Republicans. It may be the case that some Republicans are racists, and it may be that some Democrats are anti-Christian (to use some labels that have been carelessly applied recently). But both could be true of some members of the other group. It is also true that many Republicans are extraordinarily concerned that all races be treated fairly, and that many Democrats are committed and vigorous Christians. Therefore, if we use either label for the members of an entire party, we are likely bearing false witness against some of those who self-identify as Republicans or Democrats.

Of course, when speaking of groups, sometimes the use of labels does not bear false witness. If we say that Republicans nominated Donald Trump for president in 2016, or that Democrats nominated Hillary Clinton that year, we are clearly bearing true witness. But if we go on to suggest that Republicans are such-and-such kind of people because they nominated Donald Trump or that Democrats are such-and-such because they nominated Hillary Clinton, we have violated the ninth commandment. Morally loaded labels when applied to other human beings are rarely necessary.

Here is another application of this principle. What words should we use when speaking about a specific action taken by a specific person? Even if what was done is clearly defined, we should be careful about using broad category terms when not absolutely necessary. On the January 1, 2017, segment of Meet the Press, one question was whether a person should actually be labelled with the term liar, as some had done with the president. Gerard Baker, editor-in-chief of *The Wall Street Journal*, made the following very wise comment:

I'd be careful about using the word, "lie." "Lie" implies much more than just saying something that's false. It implies a deliberate intent to mislead. . . . When Donald Trump says thousands of people were on the rooftops of New Jersey on 9/11 celebrating, thousands of Muslims were there celebrating, I think it's right to investigate that claim, to report what we found, which is that nobody found any evidence of that whatsoever, and to say that.

I think it's then up to the reader to make up their own mind to say, "This is what Donald Trump says. This is what a reliable, trustworthy news organization reports. And you know what? I don't think that's true." I think if you start ascribing a moral intent, as it were, to someone by saying that they've lied, I think you run the risk that you look like you are, like you're not being objective.[2]

That final sentence is critically important. "If you start ascribing a moral intent," you are going beyond what you need to do to address what you perceive to be wrong. Baker provides no religious justification for what he says, and his understanding of the possible negative results of ascribing moral intent is purely utilitarian. But he is right to urge that we avoid the kind of labelling that ascribing moral intent invariably involves. His comments affirm one of the requirements of the ninth commandment: that we do all that we can both to stand for the truth and to do so without unnecessarily pouring condemnation on the name and the reputation of the person or persons about whom we are speaking. It is right—and necessary—to confront wrongdoing, even wrongdoing that involves nothing other than words. But Baker makes it clear that it is not necessary to apply labels.

Before I repeat my request that we eliminate the use of some labels, I would like to share some other labels that have been suggested should be banned. Most of these come from participants in an adult Sunday school class on this subject that

I taught at Calvary Presbyterian Church in Willow Grove, Pennsylvania. Others were suggested by Facebook friends in response to a couple of my posts on this subject.

Apostate
The Christian version of Boko Haram
Heterodox agitators
Feminist
Biblicist
Fundamentalist/fundie
Man-centered
Relativist

Remember, all I am suggesting is that we should consider banning these labels and phrases because they are inflammatory and unnecessary. When we disagree with certain people and positions, out of our love for God and his Word and the very people we believe need correcting, we should simply state in careful, gracious discourse the reasons for our disagreement. And the reason for considering such an action is to try to help us all live more fully in obedience to the ninth commandment.

So here is my request again: *I ask anyone who reads this book to consider talking with other Christians about the value of the specific labels I am suggesting we abandon when talking about other professing Christians. Then I suggest that you also suggest other labels that we should probably ban.*

SOCIAL MEDIA

As I was working on this book, I pondered long and hard about whether to try to address the specific challenge of bearing true witness presented by social media. Then I received the August 18, 2016, issue of *TIME* magazine and I knew I had to do so.

These words appeared on that cover: "Why We're Losing the Internet to the Culture of Hate." The cover story was titled, "How Trolls Are Ruining the Internet." The problem of how Christians speak on the internet is, of course, part of a much broader issue. What is happening on the internet challenges some of the fundamental values of modern society's entire social contract.

Hear this from Joel Stein's cover story:

> The Internet's personality has changed. Once it was a geek with lofty ideals about the free flow of information. Now, if you need help improving your upload speeds it's eager to help with the technical details, but if you tell it you're struggling with depression it will try to goad you into killing yourself. Psychologists call this the online disinhibition effect, in which factors like anonymity, invisibility, a lack of authority and not communicating in real time strip away the mores society spent millennia building. And it's seeping from our smartphones into every aspect of our lives.[3]

The "online disinhibition effect"—that in itself is a scary thought, because it suggests that both Christian norms and general societal norms seem to be easily neglected when we utilize social media. And while this effect is likely more pervasive in the general culture than in the community of professed Christians, its presence seems to be growing even in Christian communities. Who in the world would walk up to a fellow believer, whom he has just met, and call him a "jackass" to his face? Who would dream of appearing before the elders of Redeemer Presbyterian Church in New York City to accuse Tim Keller of being a heretic? Who would dare to speak personally to another Christian and say, "You're a liar, a fraud, and anti-Christian. I no longer wish to have anything to do with you because the Bible says we are not to fellowship with those who walk in darkness. Have a good day"?

The answer to these questions, of course, is no one. But I have seen all of these comments on Facebook spoken by professed Christians about other professed Christians. Is it any wonder that among the most common words found when googling "Why are Christians so . . ." are *narrow-minded, hypocritical, judgmental, mean, intolerant,* and *hateful?* While I do not want to push this analogy too far, I have to wonder whether the dechristianization of Western culture might be at least partly explained by referring back to Julian the Apostate. As noted in chapter 3, Roman Emperor Julian was able to publicly restore pagan temples in Rome because Christians were constantly at one another's throats and could not unite to oppose him. Are Christians today, by the way we talk about one another especially via social media, actually contributing to the dechristianization process? That's at least a possibility to be considered.

One of the best analyses of this problem in a specifically Christian context is that of the well-known blogger and pastor, Tim Challies. On September 26, 2018, he posted a blog entitled "The Duties Required by the Ninth Commandment in a Social Media World," and he applied to social media some of the interpretations of the ninth commandment offered by the *Westminster Larger Catechism.* Here are some questions he asks as part of his analysis:

> In what you say and what you read online, are you committed to promoting truth and to preserving and enhancing the reputation of others? Or are you willing to read rumors and innuendo? . . .

> Are you determined to stand for truth and to stand against error, not only in what you say but also in what you read? Or do you have a reputation for spreading rumors and lies? . . .

Are you committed to reading, believing, and telling only what is verifiably true? . . .

Do you demonstrate love and respect even for people with whom you disagree? Do the sites you read demonstrate that same kind of love and respect? . . .

Are you hopeful that other people will maintain a good reputation and do you rejoice in all that enhances their reputation as faithful Christians? Are you as quick to read, believe, and share information that will enhance their reputation as to tarnish it? . . .

Do you feel grief (rather than mere outrage) over the sins and weaknesses of others and a willingness to overlook their offenses (when those offenses are not so egregious that they threaten to undermine the gospel of Christ)? . . .

Do you love to receive a good report about another believer, even one with whom you have substantial disagreements? Do you refuse to receive an evil report on another believer, especially when that information is unsubstantiated or no business of yours?[4]

Another outstanding contribution toward a Christian approach to social media was shared recently by Ligon Duncan, Chancellor and CEO of Reformed Theological Seminary. He made ten brief points, and here are some of them:

> Relentlessly encourage, edify, and inform.
> Ignore trolls, mockers, and slanderers into oblivion.
> Starve dissensionists, narcissists, and errorists of the attention they crave.
> Point people to sound people and resources.
> Exalt Christ. Bible. Grace. Truth. Gospel.

Be kind. Persuade (rather than rally).
Be the same person online and offline.[5]

Here is a third example of how those concerned about the Bible's teaching on true and false witness in the arena of social media should (and should not) act has recently been provided by the Most Reverend Dr. Foley Beach, Archbishop of the Anglican Church in North America:

A Christian Code of Ethics for Using Social Media [Recommended by Dr. Foley Beach, Archbishop of the Anglican Church of North America]

Most of us have done it!! We have posted something on the Internet when we had thought, incorrectly, that we had heard all the facts. Or we have written something slamming a brother or sister in Christ personally without talking to them in person first. Or we have written something when we were in the flesh and not in the Holy Spirit that caused heartache and pain to some innocent victim of our written words. Or we have spoken prophetically only later to have wished we had shared the comments in person.

The following is a simple code of ethics (5 Questions) for the follower of Jesus to consider before one clicks the "enter" button. It is intended for the follower of Jesus to remember that even in cyber-space we are witnesses (either for good or for bad) for Jesus Christ modeling a life which is supposed to emulate him.

1. Is It the Truth?

Or is it gossip, slander, or unverified hearsay? Our responsibility is to speak truth, yet speak it in love (Ephesians 4:15). Why is it my responsibility to speak this truth, or to be judge and jury? What gives me the right to write this or post this?

2. Have I Talked to the Person before I Talk about the Person?

There is a difference between writing about what some-one has said or done and writing about the person. It is easy to speak out of our own anger and emotional needs without going to the person first. As followers of Jesus, it is not right to say anything about another person un-less it is flowing from God's love within us, and he has given us a process to do this – Matthew 18:15–20.

3. Will It Benefit All Concerned?

This is what love does. Speaking truth to another can bring benefit and repentance, but slander, hatred, and meanness bring destruction, hurt, and divisiveness in the Body. The Scriptures exhort us to avoid these kinds of things. Colossians 4:6 – Let your speech always be gracious, seasoned with salt; Ephesians 4:31 – Let all bitterness and wrath and anger and clamor and slander be put away from you, along with all malice. Be kind to one another, tenderhearted, forgiving each other as God in Christ has forgiven you.

4. Do My Words Reflect Well on Jesus Christ?

As followers of his, this is what our mission is about – sharing Jesus Christ so that others may worship Him, too. Can people see Jesus in my comments, pictures, and online activity? Do they see the fruit of the Holy Spirit being manifest in my words? 1 Corinthians 5:14 – It is the love of Christ which compels us. Am I reflecting the aroma of Christ?

5. Will I Have to Confess What I Have Written as Sin?

If so, then why write it or post it? Flee the temptation to sin.[6]

These suggestions clearly and helpfully reflect the excellent comments of Scott Sauls quoted in chapter 1.

So am I advocating that all Christians cancel their Facebook and Twitter and Instagram accounts? Not necessarily, though I often wonder whether such a mass cancellation might not produce more good than harm. Nevertheless, I think we all know that most of us won't do so. In my case, Facebook is one of the best ways for me to keep up with my grandsons, so I'm not about to cancel.

So, if not cancelling, then what? I will, with no small degree of trepidation, make some suggestions.

One, Christians especially must remember is that, no matter how sophisticated our privacy controls may seem, words used on the internet are public and permanent. In the 2016 U.S. presidential campaign, much was made of Hillary Clinton's emails when she was secretary of state. Apparently, there were ways of accessing her words even long after the emails themselves had been deleted. Of course, most of us need not fear a public leak of our emails. We just aren't worth the trouble. But the principle remains: under the right circumstances, almost anything that has ever been transmitted via the internet can be retrieved.

As unsophisticated as my internet skills are, I do know how to make a screen shot. If for some reason that doesn't work, I can block and copy to save material and then retrieve it whenever I desire. I have done that with some comments I have seen Christians make on the internet, and I still have access to those materials though the posts in question were deleted long ago. My first point, therefore, is that Christians should speak via social media platforms with the understanding that what we say might as well be etched in stone. The lesson: don't bear any witness that you don't want to be seen—even in a hundred years.

Similarly, don't bear any witness that you don't want to be seen all over the world. This is one of the amazing and exciting features of the internet—the way we can communicate around the world in the blink of an eye. In my work with the World Reformed Fellowship, I can send out a question to board members and receive answers from Seoul, Pretoria, Sydney, Edinburgh, Sao Paulo, and Jakarta within minutes. But if my question contains some false witness, it becomes public and international the instant I push the send key.

But no, many who know the internet far better than I might say. There are social media platforms which promise, and seem to deliver, at least some degree of anonymity. Of course, those who raise this point are correct. In fact, the very existence of such platforms explains, to some degree, why the internet has become "a culture of hate."

For the professing Christian, though, there is a more important consideration than whether or not our speech may be immediately exposed to the world: the fact that Jesus sees it. However effective we think some social media platform is in masking our identity, if we really believe what we say we believe, we know that he knows. And that's what really counts. The one who was and is the way, the truth, and the life will be either honored or dishonored by the way we speak. After all, he is the one who said, *"But I tell you that everyone will have to give account on the day of judgment for every empty word they have spoken. For by your words you will be acquitted, and by your words you will be condemned"* (Matthew 12:36–37).

Whatever is shared via social media platforms is included in Jesus's words.

Sometimes, however, the divine verdict on our actions and words may seem distant. This provides one explanation for the Lord's institution right here and right now of another critically important facet of our Christian lives, a fact that even appears in the *TIME* magazine analysis of the present sad state of internet morality. Remember these words: "Factors like anonymity, invisibility, a lack of authority and not communicating in real time strip away the mores society spent millennia building." In both secular and religious venues, *accountability* matters.

Jesus put it this way: "This is the verdict: Light has come into the world, but people loved darkness instead of light because their deeds were evil. Everyone who does evil hates the light, and will not come into the light for fear that their deeds will be exposed" (John 3:19–20). People loved darkness—and we still do. I know I do. All of us need to be accountable to other believers. That's as true when we speak as when we act.

And it is as true when we share something another person has written as when we write something ourselves. A good friend recently shared with me the link to a Facebook post which described in great detail how allegations of sexual abuse at a nearby church were mishandled. The original post was unstinting in its condemnation of the senior pastor of that church and, indeed, of the denomination to which the church belongs. I know that pastor quite well and I was stunned by what I read. But, for once, the fact that I have been writing this book led me to do what I believe was the right thing. I called the pastor, we set up an in-person meeting, and I had a long talk with him about the allegations in the Facebook post. I asked every hard question I could think of and, in the end, I became convinced that the original post had probably violated the ninth commandment by "speaking the truth unseasonably, or maliciously to a wrong end, or perverting it to a wrong meaning, or in doubtful or equivocal expressions, to the prejudice of the truth or justice" (*Westminster Larger Catechism* 145).

Of course, I could be wrong. My pastor-friend could have deceived me. Or perhaps more likely, I could have been blinded by my friendship with this man and refused to see the truth. Unless I personally explored the matter in detail, I could not be absolutely certain that my understanding of the situation was correct. Therefore, it would be totally inappropriate for me to post on Facebook my support for the pastor with respect to this specific situation, and I have not done so. I have received additional questions about this matter, and I have responded privately to those questions by sharing what I learned and why I think what I now do. But I will not comment publicly or in writing.

But what about the person who shared the link to the condemning post? What responsibility did the sharer bear? If the original post was wrong, then sharing the link to that post almost certainly damaged the good name of a Christian neighbor. Sharing what someone else has written is not a neutral activity. If what was originally written constitutes false witness, then sharing that material without clearly qualifying one's action may itself be false witness.

But take it a bit further. Many of us have heard horror stories about young people who committed suicide because of words about them on the internet, and studies conducted by Yale University, the Centers for Disease Control and Prevention, and other such organizations seem to confirm that there are *grounds for concern*.[7] Here is what a U.S. government website says about the subject:

> With the prevalence of social media and digital forums, comments, photos, posts, and content shared by individuals can often be viewed by strangers as well as acquaintances. The content an individual shares online—both their personal content as well as any negative, mean, or hurtful content—creates a kind of permanent public record of their views, activities, and behavior. This public record can be thought of as an online reputation, which may be accessible to schools, employers, colleges, clubs, and others who may be researching an individual now or in the future. Cyberbullying can harm the online reputations of everyone involved—not just the

person being bullied, but those doing the bullying or participating in it.[8]

There is no question that presently-available social media platforms make instant global communication quick and easy. But that, of course, has a downside. We can quickly hear reports of wrongdoing almost anywhere in the world. And we can just as quickly share those reports with others. However, we must consider the rampant problem of misrepresentations and misinterpretations. Whether we believe that words can actually create reality or simply that words can alter our perceptions of others, we need to be especially careful when we consider sharing something we have seen on one of the social media platforms if it contributes to a negative perception of another person. For example, it may be right for a person who has been sexually abused to speak out, even in public, about that experience. And it may be right for the person accused to speak back, even in public. But unless we have detailed, first-hand knowledge of the situation, we should certainly avoid commenting on it, especially on public social media platforms.

For all of these and many others reasons, I suggest that Christian organizations and churches pay more attention to what their members say on the internet. The seventh commandment forbidding adultery continues to attract a lot of attention, as well it should in our current environment. But that same environment seems to demand that at least as much attention be paid to how Christians, including Christian leaders, speak via various forms of social media. Living in full obedience to *all* that our God has commanded requires great care and thoughtfulness. Nowhere is that more the case than when we speak, especially when we speak via an internet platform. That is why many churches and religious organizations have adopted detailed social media policies and guidelines. One of these is printed in the first appendix to this book, and I strongly commend this biblical guidance to my readers. It seems wise for all of us to consider carefully what guidelines we will follow in our online postings.

THE ROLE OF THE CHURCH

I have spoken above about the fact that labels likely lie.

But sometimes there really is *poison* in a bottle labelled poison. Occasionally, there is spiritual "poison" in individuals who call themselves Christians—at least, this seems to be what the apostle Paul suggests in Galatians 1:6–9.

> I am astonished that you are so quickly deserting the one who called you to live in the grace of Christ and are turning to a different gospel— which is really no gospel at all. Evidently some people are throwing you into confusion and are trying to pervert the gospel of Christ. But even if we or an angel from heaven should preach a gospel other than the one we preached to you, let them be under God's curse! As we have already said, so now I say again: If anybody is preaching to you a gospel other than what you accepted, let them be under God's curse!

So when error must be confronted, we should certainly do that. But we should, as appropriate, do it by *consulting the church*.

Before I delve into the reasons for and methods of consulting the church, I need to provide a further qualification. This particular rule works only when we become convinced that another Christian is clearly outside the bounds of how that person's church defines proper belief and behavior. The need for this qualification should be obvious. To take a real but (thankfully) now outdated example, if a church were to officially affirm apartheid, there would be no grounds for me to appeal to that church about one of its members who supported apartheid. That member would be living consistently with the stated position of the church, so discipline by that church would not be a recourse, sadly, in that case.

However, many of the accusations hurled at Christians come from other Christians who do share their same official, church standards. When this is the case, the church of the one being accused becomes exceedingly important. At least it does if we believe that the church really is part of God's plan for his people.

So long as we avoid labels and heed cautions such as those we saw given by Jonathan Edwards, vigorous debates are completely appropriate and usually very helpful, both to the participants and even to the broader church. But we must recognize that occasions can arise when we believe that a professed Christian is violating the scriptural standards in faith or life adopted by his or her own church. How do we proceed when we come to that conclusion? That is when we must consult the church.

In chapter 2, I discussed catechisms of a variety of churches. That was intentional. While I did not include a lot of churches, I tried to mention the confessional commitments of a number of them not only to show commonality in truth-telling but also in order to emphasize my understanding of the critically important role the church should play in all of these matters.

Throughout Scripture, the "body-ness" of the Christian community is emphasized over and over. One of the most obvious is Paul's letter to the church, the body of Christ, in Ephesus. Here are some key passages (emphasis added). I realize it's a long list, but that is precisely the point.

> In him *the whole building* is joined together and rises to become *a holy temple* in the Lord. And in him you too are being built together to become a *dwelling* in which God lives by his Spirit. (Ephesians 2:21–22, note how *building*, *temple*, and *dwelling* are all singular nouns)

> This mystery is that through the gospel the Gentiles are heirs together with Israel, members together of

one body, and sharers together in the promise in Christ Jesus. (Ephesians 3:6)

Make every effort to keep the *unity* of the Spirit through the bond of peace. There is *one body* and one Spirit, just as you were called to one hope when you were called; *one Lord, one faith, one baptism; one God and Father of all,* who is over all and through all and in all. (Ephesians 4:3–6)

. . . to equip his people for works of service, so that *the body* of Christ may be built up until we all reach unity in the faith and in the knowledge of the Son of God and become mature, attaining to the whole measure of the fullness of Christ. (Ephesians 4:12–13)

Therefore each of you must put off falsehood and speak truthfully to your neighbor, for we are all members of *one body*. (Ephesians 4:25, note the link between speak ing truthfully and *one body*)

Get rid of all bitterness, rage and anger, brawling and slander, along with every form of malice. Be kind and compassionate to one another, forgiving each other, just as in Christ God forgave you. (Ephesians 4:31–32)

Let no one deceive you with empty words, for because of such things God's wrath comes on those who are disobedient. (Ephesians 5:6, notice the link between empty words and disobedience)

The emphasis on a united church body is hard for most of us who live in Western cultures to appreciate, and examining its full background and scope would require another book. But let me try to put just a bit of flesh on the dry bones of my assertion.

Americans generally tend to be freedom-loving and individualistic in our mind-sets. One of the best books ever written

about the American Revolution is Bernard Bailyn's *The Ideological Origins of the American Revolution*,[9] a book so good it
was awarded both the Pulitzer Prize and the Bancroft Prize for
American history. Bailyn describes a "contagion of liberty"—
how the notion of the absolute freedom of the individual came
to pervade all of American society in the years just before and
after the Revolution.[10]

And I do mean all of society. In his analysis, Bailyn quotes
as many sermons as he does any other source. It is no surprise
that Unitarianism flourished and churches lost their establishment influence during these years.

I do not believe that everything American is Christian.
Further, I believe the attitude toward personal freedom that
was built into the American psyche (and constitution) is not
equivalent to the understanding of freedom in Scripture. The
American understanding is primarily a freedom *from* anyone
telling me what to do, while the scriptural understanding is
primarily a freedom to worship God as he deserves.[11]

Few American theologians have taken seriously the degree
to which our view of the world and of the Christian faith has
been radically shaped by the colonial "contagion of liberty."
One of the areas that has been most profoundly contagion-
shaped is our understanding of the nature of the church, especially the degree to which we recognize and submit to the
authority of any church.

If the church is what most of us believe it to be—the body
of our Lord Jesus Christ—then it must have a place in our conversation about other Christians, especially when we disagree
with those Christians about matters of faith or life. As John
Calvin has said, echoing many others past and present, we
"should yield to the church the authority it deserves."[12]

Of course, in our pluralistic world, there are thousands of
specific manifestations of "the church." Some individuals have
taken this to mean that, because there is no one global church,

all specific churches can be ignored whenever we choose to do so. I suggest that doing so violates the spirit, if not the direct teaching, of the passages from Ephesians quoted above. I believe that the "contagion of liberty" has led us to think and act largely as Lone Rangers whenever the spirit—not always the Holy Spirit—moves us.

I have mentioned people concerned about the teaching of Pastor Tim Keller. Certainly, those with such concerns should be able to follow up on those concerns. But they need first to avoid lying labels, second to realize the potential for both good and bad of social media, and third to yield to the church the authority it deserves.

What exactly might it mean to give due authority to the church in this situation? Keller is a minister in the Presbyterian Church in America, and that church proclaims its commitment to the historic gospel of truth once delivered to the saints. Instead of broadcasting claims about his errors to the world, the author should first contact Keller to communicate his concerns. If the pastor does not provide a satisfactory response, the author should make a formal complaint to his ruling elders. If there is no satisfactory response from them, the matter should be brought to the presbytery where Keller is a member and is accountable. All of this should occur before making any public statements, either with or without labels. This is the least that should be done in cases like this, to yield to the church the authority it deserves.

"But that would take so much time," someone might argue. "His elders are his friends; they wouldn't listen! His presbytery is far too busy to be bothered by what a single person thinks about one pastor. Therefore, I will just blast away, knowing that I will never be held accountable for what I say. I have free speech and I'm going to use it." I suggest that this is a common, if largely subconscious, attitude in many hearts. But it is contrary to what Jesus means when he says, "If you hold to my teaching, you are really my disciples. Then you will know the truth, and the truth will set you free" (John 8:31–32).

One final and critically important point needs to be made with respect to the church. According to Scripture, it is the church that has the responsibility to speak publicly about sins it has identified among its members and in society at large. In some cases, the speaking will be done by a local congregation. In other cases, it will be an entire denomination or group of churches. While such ecclesiastical responsibility is largely outside the scope of this book, it needs to be affirmed here. Sin must not be ignored. As both God the Father and Jesus the Son spoke words of judgment when sin was revealed, so must the biblically ordained church speak when sin is revealed. However, precisely because no church is itself infallible, great care must be taken when such speaking occurs.

Numerous groups and agencies have sought to provide guidelines for such speaking. The details of legal requirements, investigative procedures, evidence gathering, and corroborative requirements must be developed carefully and made public both within and outside the specific churches. Churches are as responsible to show the same concern for the good names of its members as are individual Christians. But churches and other Christian organizations may occasionally find it necessary to speak publicly about sin that has been identified in their midst. The World Reformed Fellowship has sought to gather suggestions about these matters from around the world, and has posted the results on its website. To learn how to find these documents online, see the first appendix of this book.

And perhaps most important of all, whatever policies a specific church or Christian organization adopts must be publicly available and required reading for all of its employees.

CHRISTIAN COLLEGES AND SEMINARIES

Suppose a Christian college or seminary comes to believe that one of its faculty members has moved outside the boundaries of the faith commitments of the school. Such an institution has the right and obligation to explore that matter thoroughly. After all, when a Christian school makes a public declaration that it stands for certain truths, the ninth commandment requires that it do everything in its power to uphold those truths. So a full exploration of any perceived deviation is not only appropriate, but mandatory.

But yielding to the church the authority it deserves should also be part of the process if the school and the faculty member's church hold the same beliefs on the matter in question. Considering the church always means consulting the church. At the very least, the seminary must do that consulting before publicly speaking any words or taking actions which might, in any way, damage or raise questions about the good name of a Christian neighbor or our Savior.

Again, we must take into account the religious pluralism which so dominates our church culture. This makes things more complex. It also makes full truth-telling more difficult, just as many of God's other requirements for his people make life more complex. But obedience to God's word is not waived just because it is difficult. In some ways, costly obedience brings even more honor to our Lord than easy obedience. That's because costly obedience more clearly reveals that we have no other god than the Lord.

Let's go back to the seminary example and see how such a process of church consultation might work. Suppose a seminary comes to believe that one of its faculty members has moved outside the boundaries of the faith or life commitments of the school. What should the school do? If private discussions with the faculty member fail to resolve the issue and if the school and the professor are part of the same church, the school should privately discuss the matter with the appropriate church authorities. (Of course, this type of procedure must be spelled out in the employment contracts of the school.) Because the church and the school are different parts of the same body, this is clearly the correct course of action. The church deserves the opportunity to have input into the process that might result in the dismissal of one of its members from teaching service, and the church can help the school to make sure that what the school says about the faculty member is true witness. However, the church and the school might come to different conclusions about the faculty member. In that case, if anything is said publicly about the faculty member, both the church and the school should clearly state their reasons for differences with the other. That way, the whole truth will be told and the witness borne will be true.

Suppose, however, that the school is not an official part of the church to which the faculty member belongs but both the school and the church have the same theological standards on the immediate issue. What then? Yes, it is more complex, but remember that biblical obedience is not always simple or easy. If there is just one body of Christ—and there is!—and if both the faculty member and the school claim to be part of that body, there will be some appropriate way to involve official church representatives. At that point, my suggestions in the previous paragraph apply. The principle is: don't ignore the church. Consult the church, listen to the church and allow the advice of the church to be a safeguard against the danger of bearing false witness.

A quick (but very painful) example: As I have mentioned, in 2003 I was told by the board of trustees of Westminster Theological Seminary that I should consider how I was guilty of shading the truth and thus bearing false witness. It was absolutely imperative, in my judgment, that the church to which I was accountable be consulted about this matter. And it was. I am an ordained teaching elder in the Orthodox Presbyterian Church and am directly accountable to the presbytery of New York and New England. The ministerial relations committee received a full report of this action and participated in an extensive follow-up process. This was done even though there is no official connection between Westminster and that denomination. It was done because both the seminary and the denomination affirm the same doctrinal statements and because this is what it means to consult and to yield to the church the authority it deserves.

The process plays out somewhat differently if the school and the church to which the faculty member belongs do not share the same theological and ethical commitments. In such a situation, if the faculty member is living consistently within the standards of his or her church, the most that consulting with that church might accomplish would be a better understanding between the church and the school. But even that might lessen the possibility of any false witness. Therefore, while not obligatory, it probably is a wise thing to do.

My main point, however, applies primarily when all involved share the same theological and ethical standards. And that, I must say, is precisely the situation in which problems seem most often to arise.

When appropriately consulted, the church where the person being accused is a member has both the opportunity and the responsibility to exercise what Greg Gilbert calls, "defensive protection" of the good name of Jesus. Gilbert explains, "This happens when a church has to say to one of its members, 'Now, your life doesn't look like a Christian's, and if you're going to hang on to your sin and forsake Christ, we can't let you go on living like that while calling yourself a Christian.' In other words, the church invalidates or disaffirms that individual's claim of being a Christian. Historically, that action has been called church discipline."[13]

The church's authority may be spiritual, but it is real nonetheless, and we deny the power of the passages from Ephesians if we don't recognize that authority in word and deed.

Some of these suggestions may seem radical—and they may be radical! It is even possible that they are radically *wrong*. I simply urge that their rightness or wrongness be decided on the basis of biblical teaching, not on the basis of expediency. Because they are made up of people, Christian colleges and seminaries and other kinds of Christian organizations are as likely as any individual to be infected by the "contagion of liberty." Yielding to the church the authority it deserves is a biblical antidote to that contagion.

All of us in the West (certainly including myself) have been affected by this "contagion of liberty." When we see a problem we think needs to be addressed, we are eager to exercise our perceived "freedom" to address it in any way we see fit. We want to be free *from* any restraints which might restrict the way or the timing of our public discourse. There are, of course, libel laws that place secular restraints on our speech. Perhaps we ought to consider whether there are any divine laws—restraints we should welcome—that also place restraints on our speech. We should consider these laws because they are designed to make us free to bring uncompromised glory to the good name of our God.

In this chapter, I have suggested some specific guidelines that I believe will help Christians live in full obedience to the ninth commandment. In the next chapter, I will apply these guidelines to specific and current areas of controversy.

5.

SO CAN WE TALK AT ALL?

We face many challenges when we speak. In light of all that I have said, some may feel that it is impossible to speak correctly and may be inclined either to keep quiet or just to blast away.

Indeed, when I posted some online articles on this subject, one church leader responded, "I don't know how we can have discussions of anything with your understanding of what is required by the WLC's (*Westminster Larger Catechism*'s) exposition of the ninth commandment." Such a perception must not be lightly dismissed. As with any area of the Christian life, obedience takes work—sometimes very hard and time-consuming work. Protecting and promoting the good name of my Christian neighbor and the good name of my Savior often requires great care and great effort.

In the fall of 2017, a diverse group of Christian evangelicals met in New York City to discuss the problem of verbal nastiness among Christians. Very quickly, that group came to the conclusion that civility without a recognition of injustice and error would be worse than the nastiness which was the announced reason for the gathering. A document titled "Some Thoughts on Christian Civility" was produced. Endorsed unanimously by the executive committee of the World Reformed Fellowship, it has been reproduced with permission in the first appendix to this book. It provides a clear example of how important and divisive issues can be addressed without any violation of the ninth commandment.

In this chapter, I will make some specific suggestions about several issues that divide Christians today: abortion, evolution, women in church leadership roles, social justice matters, and same-sex marriage. I will also make brief comments about accusations of sexual impropriety by Christians. Of course, I will not seek to resolve any of the debates about these issues. I will simply suggest ways to avoid bearing false witness when we engage in legitimate and critically important discussion of issues on which we disagree. If the suggestions I make are at all helpful, the principles involved may be applied to any areas in which Christians disagree with one another.

FOUR PRELIMINARY MATTERS

Before proceeding to the specific discussions, however, I would like to make four preliminary points. Each is a principle to apply when discussing issue on which we disagree.

Point 1: Our Words Matter

First, let's take a closer look at Matthew 12, where Jesus warns that everyone will have to account for empty words they have spoken. As always, context matters. Jesus's public ministry caused both jubilation and hatred, and these produce a major confrontation in this chapter. After Jesus healed a man on the Sabbath, the crowds swarmed him, and he healed many of them (v. 15). "Then they brought him a demon-possessed man who was blind and mute, and Jesus healed him, so that he could both talk and see. All the people were astonished and said, 'Could this be the Son of David?'" (vv. 22–23). Yes, of course it could be—and it was!

Not everyone saw things this way. "But when the Pharisees heard this, they said, 'It is only by Beelzebul, the prince of demons, that this fellow drives out demons'" (v. 24). Jesus's response to the Pharisees concludes with this powerful statement:

> "You brood of vipers, how can you who are evil say anything good? For the mouth speaks what the heart is full of. A good man brings good things out of the good stored up in him, and an evil man brings evil things out of the evil stored up in him. But I tell you that everyone will have to give account on the day of judgment for every empty word they have spoken. For by your words you will be acquitted, and by your words you will be condemned." (Matthew 12:34–37, emphasis added)

No, Jesus is not repudiating the doctrine of justification by faith alone. However, he is making abundantly clear that our speech matters. Both the words and the condition of the heart in which the speech originates have huge and possibly eternal consequences. The Pharisees had first questioned Jesus about the man healed on the Sabbath, and Jesus responded with a clear and specific answer. It is okay to ask questions. And, when those questions are asked without the use of lying labels, they can be answered simply and directly. But labeling Jesus a disciple of Beelzebul crosses a line, just as our labelling a minister in good standing a heretic crosses a line.

To stay on the right side of the God-honoring line while still raising necessary questions and concerns takes work. But such work does bring honor to our Lord, and nothing is more important than that.

Point 2: Check Your Motive

My second preliminary point is that we must remember to act out of love. Paul wrote, "If I speak in the tongues of men and angels, but do not have love, I am only a resounding gong or a clanging symbol" (1 Corinthians 13:1). And Jesus said, "You have heard that it was said, 'Love your neighbor and hate your enemy.' But I tell you, love your enemies and pray for those who persecute you, that you may be children of your Father in heaven. He causes his sun to rise on the evil and the good, and sends rain on the righteous and the unrighteous" (Matthew 5:43–45).

If we genuinely love those with whom we disagree, we will desire more than anything else that they come to the truth and, in that truth, find the blessings of God. The lesson of Jonah must always remain uppermost in our mind when we are conversing about or with those whom we think are wrong. Jonah seemed to detest the fact that the Ninevites to whom he preached repented in response to God's word. But to borrow from God's words to Jonah, should we not have great concern for those whom we believe are wrong? Should not our speech to and about them express not just disagreement but also loving concern?

Before, during, and after we speak any words of disagreement, we need to make sure our most fundamental motive is love.

We must not bear false witness, especially when communicating about a matter on which we disagree with other Christians. This is where I have placed most of my emphasis thus far. What words can we use that are most likely to communicate truth with gracious concern, or with a clear ultimate purpose of leading my antagonist to the joy and blessing of the truth? If we think other people are actually Ninevites, do we speak to or about them in ways that push them toward the judgment we think they deserve? Or do we find ways of speaking which are most likely, in the power of the Holy Spirit, to attract them to the truth? This is what I believe is meant by "speaking the truth in love" (Ephesians 4:15).

Yes, it is challenging to try to speak hard things in love. But that, of course, is exactly what God did for us in Christ. And that is what he offers us the opportunity to do for others.

Point 3: Stay on Point and Cast No Aspersions

My third point follows directly from the first two. We should stay on point when discussing the issues and, as appropriate, discuss them vigorously. But *we should never cast aspersions on the intelligence, or the theological orthodoxy, or the moral standing of the professed Christians with whom we are disagreeing.*

I remember vividly one painful public exchange in which I participated. I had expressed my personal support for Douglas Green in his exposition of what he and others call "Christotelic hermeneutics." In simple terms, this concerns the degree to which the human authors of Scripture understood the specific details of how the messianic prophecies they uttered would be fulfilled.[1]

Of course, complexity surrounds this highly technical subject. But in response to my comments, one professed Christian said in a Facebook post that my opinion should carry no weight because of my "liberal politics" and "obsequious" relationship with one of my sons. The Christian posting this message may certainly have been correct in saying that I was wrong in my approach to Scripture. And I suppose that someone could accuse me of being liberal politically, depending on how they define it. I also may very well have been a bad parent. But I do not see a clear and necessary connection between either of these characteristics and Christotelic hermeneutics. Perhaps there is a connection. But if there is, staying on point requires that this connection be clearly made.

If a hermeneutical method does in fact compromise some aspect of Scripture, and the ninth commandment requires standing against it for the sake of truth, does labelling one of its supporters "liberal" and "obsequious" represent the best way to obey that commandment? I contend that it does not. Actually, using this kind of language probably undermines more than it supports the speaker's stand for the truth.

Finally, if the personal charges against me are correct, the role of the church, mentioned in the last chapter, becomes relevant. Public statements about any person's character or theological orthodoxy should be shared *first* with the relevant judicatory of that person's church if the church and those making the accusations affirm the same theological and ethical standards.

Another way of saying this is to insist that, in *every* circumstance of expressing disagreement with another Christian, we all must concentrate our words on the issue and not on the character of the person who has made what we believe to be an error. Even in doing so, however, we must avoid using lazy labels. Saying that another person's ideas are "stupid" or "uninformed" or even "liberal" or "fundamentalist" accomplishes nothing to furthering understanding and communication.

Point 4: Secure Slippery Slopes

My fourth and final preliminary point is more technical but no less important than the first three. In our conversations about matters on which there is disagreement, we must clearly and openly take account of what are often called slippery slopes.[2]

Frequently, disagreements over the teachings of Scripture seem to focus not so much on a specific position but on what is perceived to be the inevitable conclusion to which that position may lead. Such perceptions may indeed be correct, and we must always consider that possibility. But first, I want to acknowledge that there is an inherent danger in making any slippery slope argument.

Most obviously, any such argument involves using human reason to determine the direction a certain position must or probably will lead. Certainly, we must use our minds; that's why the Lord gave us minds. But just as certainly, our minds have limits of finitude and of sinful corruption. Recognizing those limits is absolutely essential, no matter which slippery slope we think someone else may be on.

Simply stated, many of the points on which we disagree with other Christians have to do with eternal and infinite matters. In trying to understand these matters, we should expect that we will reach a point beyond which our minds simply cannot go, at least not in this life. Take, for example, the age-old apparent dichotomy of human responsibility versus divine sovereignty. If we push either side of this dichotomy too hard, opponents can claim that we are on a slippery slope to some unbiblical place. While we do need to be careful when we discuss divine sovereignty and human responsibility, to affirm either does not necessarily mean we are on a slippery slope to some heretical place.

It is not appropriate to dismiss a person's point just because one might follow that line of reasoning to an extreme conclusion. We should focus on the position a person is taking and not on where either that person or someone else might end up.

On the other hand, every speaker and writer who is concerned about communicating accurately and truthfully needs to recognize slippery slopes. Almost every statement we make about divine and eternal things will have a potential slippery slope component somewhere. Therefore, we must think carefully about where the argument we are making could go. And, if one of those places is unbiblical, we must be certain to do all that we can to make it clear that we don't mean for it to go there. We must also take the time to show how and why our argument does not go where it could go.

To give a specific example from the history of theology, I return to my favorite theologian, Jonathan Edwards. In his *Treatise on the Freedom of the Will*, Edwards makes the strongest argument I have ever read in support, ironically, of the *bondage* of the will. A huge portion of that treatise focuses on his response to objections to the position he is taking. Most of those objections are of the slippery slope variety. If one takes the position Edwards takes, the argument goes, one must be on a slippery slope to absolute determinism in which human beings have no responsibility for anything. In fact, some critics claimed Edwards was on the same philosophical and theological path as the ancient Greek stoic philosophers.[3]

In Edwards's case, it was absolutely essential to show that the determinism of the Greek Stoics was not a necessary outcome of his belief in divine sovereignty, and he had to secure that potentially very slippery slope. He certainly gave that a massive effort. One may claim that he did not succeed, but one cannot argue that he ignored his securing responsibility. In his treatise, he spends roughly half his time attempting to demonstrate that he understands and addresses the possible slippery slope his basic position could slide down. In this regard, he seems to fulfill his responsibilities under the ninth commandment. And we should follow his example if we genuinely want to make sure that our words are appropriately secured from going down any possible slippery slopes.

Of course, there may be times our disagreement with others who claim the name of Christ is fierce. Certainly, this is true for me when it comes to some of the potential views I will bring up in this chapter. We may believe such views are dangerous to the church. We may believe they undermine the Bible so fully that they require drastic action, including that we separate from those who persist in teaching those errors. But none of this means we are allowed to break the ninth commandment. Even when separating from other Christians, we must be utterly truthful about them, eager to rejoice in any good reports about them, and careful not to present our own views in ways that are needlessly offensive. I don't want to minimize the seriousness with which we are to treat error, but I do want to encourage us to think seriously and biblically about how to talk about those disagreements in the public square.

These are my preliminary points. Now I want to show how we might use them when we discuss some specific controversies that arise among evangelical, Bible-believing Christians. I personally believe that the Bible is absolutely authoritative in all that it teaches and I will begin each discussion of how to disagree in a Christ-honoring manner about specific controversial topics by sharing my own understanding of what Scripture teaches on those subjects. This is what I mean when I write about "my convictions" or "my belief." I do this because the reader deserves to know what I believe before I suggest how to discuss our differences.[4]

ABORTION

What do I believe the Bible teaches about abortion?

I believe that, according to Scripture, God has made all human beings in his own image and that, for this very reason, human life must never be taken without just cause. This, it seems to me, is the sense of Genesis 9:6. "Whoever sheds human blood, by humans shall their blood be shed; for in the image of God has God made mankind." Of course, many who decline to recognize any special authority in Scripture also deny human life is special. But I am purposely seeking to address Christians for whom the Bible is authoritative.

Secure Slippery Slopes

Even those who grant special authority to Genesis 9:6 may immediately sense two slippery slope possibilities in what I say the Bible teaches. The first involves the phrase *just cause*. A full discussion of this issue would take us into examinations of both war and capital punishment. If I were discussing this subject with someone who supported the availability of abortion, I would have to clarify why the phrase *human life must not be taken without just cause* does not necessarily involve prohibiting all war and capital punishment.

The second potential slippery slope in my statement has to do with the word *human*. What exactly does this word mean in the context of the biblical command? The many possible definitions of this word become relevant in a discussion about the morality of abortion. I would need to show how my position that human life must not be taken without just cause applies to severely brain-injured individuals or to comatose individuals or to any others whose physical or mental abilities seem to be severely compromised.

Conversely, one who believes that the Bible does not prohibit abortion would need to deal with such potential slippery slopes as the cut-off date for abortion and the exact severity of in-utero distress which would justify abortion. They would also need to address the possibility of the infanticide of deformed or unwanted babies. And, depending on the grounds cited in their support for abortion, they might need to clarify how their position does or does not relate to capital punishment and military violence.

Stay on Point and Cast No Aspersions

No matter what one's personal beliefs may be, conversations with or about other Christians on the Bible's teaching about abortion should avoid the common labels of *pro-life* and *pro-choice*. Why? Because both labels can be misleading, even when used by people of themselves. They are both "doubtful or equivocal expressions," to use the terminology of the Westminster Larger Catechism. Someone who calls himself pro-life is, by inference, suggesting that that his opponent is pro-death. Our belief may be that an abortion results in the death of a human being. But when we talk to or about another Christian whose beliefs about scriptural teaching are different from ours, we must avoid making comments about their moral standing. Discuss the position, not the person, and avoid equivocal expressions.

The same holds true for those who believe the Bible allows abortions. They should avoid the term *pro-choice* because it suggests that those who disagree with them want to force their will upon pregnant women and, by inference, on anyone who doesn't agree with them about anything. While those who take the opposite position do seek to prohibit abortions, they generally do not want to remove choice totally from either their lives or the lives of others. Discuss the position, not the person, and avoid equivocal expressions.

Another term which ought to be avoided when discussing abortion is the word *rights*. First, the mind-set that tends to lie behind that word, especially in a country founded amidst a "contagion of liberty," is not easy to find in Scripture. Several times in the book of Acts, the rights of Roman citizens create a discussion of whether the treatment Paul endured was legal. But in those and other cases, rights were asserted only as a means of remaining free to preach the gospel.

Further, in 1 Corinthians 9, Paul repeatedly affirms that even if he could claim rights, as an apostle he would not do so: "But I have not used any of these rights. And I am not writing this in the hope that you will do such things for me, for I would rather die than allow anyone to deprive me of this boast" (v. 15). Then again, "What then is my reward? Just this: that in preaching the gospel I may offer it free of charge, and so not make full use of my rights as a preacher of the gospel" (v. 18).

Even more significant for this study, the notion of rights is at least as controversial as the notion of when a fetus becomes a human being. Discussions about abortion which involve the assertion of rights often end up being a kind of shouting match over whether the rights of the fetus take precedence over the rights of the mother. And that leads nowhere.

The Good Name

So how should we focus our discussions about and with other Christians with whom we disagree on the subject of abortion? Certainly, study the Scriptures which seem to address the issue, and when possible, use studies which discuss the subject carefully. Among such studies are Joni Eareckson Tada's *Life in the Balance*, which is opposed to abortion,[6] and materials produced by the Religious Coalition for Reproductive Choice, which are supportive of abortion.[7]

The disagreement which led to your raising this subject with a Christian friend may never produce complete agreement. But conversations about the subject can be conducted in ways that genuinely bear true witness.

And they may do much more if we allow them to.

Both sides need to give adequate attention to the whole range of issues which surround abortion. By both our actions and our words, we should make clear that we are concerned not just about a political victory, but about every need related to the issue. That's where conversations will produce the most good.

A good example of this is a document that circulated during the 2016 U.S. presidential campaign, and I commend that document to all of us. It was written by fifteen leading evangelicals and was entitled "Public Faith: A Christian Voice for the Common Good." Here is what that document said about abortion:

> We have seen the culture wars rage over the issue of abortion for the past forty years with results that have been at turns life-affirming and toxic. We have no interest in the politicization of abortion for partisan gain. But we find that scripture, biology and the demands of human dignity require a societal response to the tragedy of abortion and the popular rhetoric that either needlessly inflames and offends or rationalizes away our responsibility to act at all. Towards that end, we believe that abortion must be opposed holistically, from

114

the economic patterns that often drive the practice to the societal values that justify it. This includes caring for mothers throughout motherhood, advocating for adoption, and other policies that treat mothers, babies, and other family members as those made in the image of God.[8]

A recent brief statement reflecting these kinds of concerns was made by Matt Chandler, Pastor of The Village Church in Texas:

As the Church, we must not say of abortion, "This is murder," without saying to pregnant women, "We will serve you." If we're doing the former without the latter, we aren't truly understanding the gospel.[9]

Pope Francis made a similar point in his apostolic exhortation, "Gaudete et Exsultate," issued in 2018: "Our defense of the innocent unborn, for example, needs to be clear, firm and passionate. Equally sacred, however, are the lives of the poor, those already born, the destitute, the abandoned and the underprivileged, the vulnerable infirm and elderly exposed to covert euthanasia, the victims of human trafficking, new forms of slavery, and every form of rejection."[10]

Whatever words we speak, either in support of or in opposition to abortion, must be spoken out of a total commitment to ministering to all of the needs of human beings. Remember the power of words to create action. In much the same way, actions often "speak."[11] Those who oppose abortion must make certain that their churches welcome and care for mothers and their babies born out of wedlock. A couple I know has served as foster parents for twenty-eight such children, a remarkable example of such care focused especially on the babies.

Likewise, those who support abortion must demonstrate holistic care for pregnant women and that includes women who choose to bear their children and children who are born into difficult circumstances. For example, suppose a pregnant woman is told that it is highly likely that her child will suffer from Down's Syndrome and she chooses to go ahead with the birth. Those who had counselled her toward abortion may at that point be tempted to turn away with a Jonah-like "told-you-so" attitude. Yielding to such a temptation would be contrary to all that Scripture teaches about Christian attitudes toward children.

Matthew Parris is a columnist for *The Times* (Scotland, UK) and he takes the opposite position from the positions I take on almost every ethical issue. In 2018, he published an editorial entitled "Abortion Triumphalism Is Deeply Troubling." He was responding to a vote in Ireland that dramatically loosened the restrictions on abortion in that country. He supported that decision, but he lamented the way supporters of both sides in the debate had demonized those who took a different position. Here are his words:

> But in the response that victory has met from the winning side on this as well as on the other shore of the Irish Sea, there has been a shaft of anger, contempt, and disbelief that anyone could take a different view. I'm noticing intolerance more widely than just in this debate on abortion: on gay rights; on adoption; on the MeToo movement and the issue of sexual consent, on the status of trans people . . . all areas where sometimes one may take the liberal and sometimes the conservative view, but in every case should acknowledge that these are genuinely difficult questions on which it is possible honestly and in good faith to reach differing conclusions.[12]

This is the spirit in which Christians should express their disagreement with others, with respect to abortion and with respect to all of the other issues which frequently divide us.

Check Your Motive

I now come to my most important point. I strongly recommend that, whatever position one has taken on the abortion issue, the following question should be asked in some form: "If, in the end, I cannot come to agree with you on this subject, what would you most like to see from me and others who take my position?" That is, of course, the form in which the question should be asked if the dialogue has been directly between two disagreeing parties. In a public forum, in an article or a review or a social media post, the question might take this form, "If I continue to hold the position I have expressed, what legitimate concerns of the other side should I be sure to try to address in my future words and deeds?"

While such a question might be outside the specific scope of the ninth commandment, it does relate to what was said in chapter 1 about how language creates reality. How we express our disagreements surely creates a kind of reality, and this kind of question—if asked sincerely—does so even more. We may not be able to do exactly what the other party desires. But asking the question communicates our concern for the person with whom we disagree. If the discussion is a personal one and we ask the question directly, the answer we get may provide the most important information we gain from the conversation. If the discussion is more public, forcing ourselves to express the valid concerns of the other position may provide more insight than everything else we have said. At the very least, our asking will communicate that all Christians are in this together instead of in some kind of Manichean, dualistic universe with all the "right" Christians in one realm and all the "wrong" Christians in a separate—and obviously inferior—

realm. Such unity would provide an extraordinary biblical testimony to the watching world.

EVOLUTION

Evolution is another hot topic—and another which seems frequently to produce extraordinarily nasty language among professing Christians.

I said that I will make clear what I believe the Bible teaches about each issue I discuss so that readers will know my beliefs. I believe that the essential point the Bible makes in Genesis 1 through 3 is that God created all that exists. No matter how long he took and no matter what kinds of processes he did or did not use, "In the beginning, God created the heavens and the earth" (Genesis 1:1). I am thus absolutely convinced that he created everything that exists. And, because of this fact alone, everything that exists owes him complete obedience and worship. I have read wildly divergent theories of how God did his creative work. But, possibly because I just don't know enough Hebrew grammar or enough about how the early chapters of Genesis do and do not reflect other traditions in the ancient Near East, or enough about the relevant biological or physical sciences, or enough mathematics regarding what is possible and not possible about the length of time the earth may have existed, I just have not been able to come to a final conclusion about the creative process which the Lord used. I suppose this is just as much a position as any other. And my reader deserves to know this.

Stay on Point and Cast No Aspersions

Once when I raised a question about the possible future trajectory of the evolutionary process with a Christian proponent of evolution, I was called delusional. And I often see words like *ignorant* and *morons* used to describe those who question the theory of evolution. On the other side, Christians who believe that the theory of evolution is wrong can be tempted to label those with whom they disagree as *non-Christian*, *liberal*, *arrogant*, *intellectually dishonest*, or worse. In both cases, I have heard language like this used by self-professed Christians about other self-professed Christians. Brothers and sisters, this should not be!

Based on my many communications both with those evangelical Christians who accept some form of the theory of evolution and those evangelicals who oppose all forms of that theory, most genuinely do seem to agree on the essential point I mentioned above—that God created everything that exists. Therefore, I urge that conversations about this subject also begin there. What exactly does it mean to affirm that God created all that is? What difference must that fact make in our lives? And then, more painfully, what difference is it actually making in your life? To use Francis Schaeffer's penetrating words, "How should we then live"[13] if God is the Creator of the heavens and the earth? How should we care for the bodies God has created? How should we care for the earth he has created? How should we worship? How should we serve both the Creator and other human beings whom he created? Yes, of course, these questions will also lead to differences, and those will need to be explored. But finding a common starting point can be exceptionally useful for making sure that how we discuss our differences about the length of the creation process conform to the requirements of the ninth commandment.

To understand the importance of starting here, consider how Scripture makes acknowledging the Creator a starting point for a whole life of obedience and faith.

> They are corrupt and not his children;
>> to their shame they are a warped and crooked generation.

Is this the way you repay the Lord,
   you foolish and unwise people?
Is he not your Father, your Creator,
   who made you and formed you? (Deuteronomy 32:5–6)

Why do you complain, Jacob?
   Why do you say, Israel,
"My way is hidden from the Lord;
   my cause is disregarded by my God"?
Do you not know?
   Have you not heard?
The Lord is the everlasting God,
   the Creator of the ends of the earth.
He will not grow tired or weary,
   and his understanding no one can fathom.
He gives strength to the weary
   and increases the power of the weak. (Isaiah 40:27–29)

They exchanged the truth about God for a lie, and worshiped and served created things rather than the Creator—who is forever praised. (Romans 1:25)

In these and other passages, God makes abundantly clear the essential lessons he wants us to learn from the beginning of Genesis. No affirmation of the truth of that passage of Scripture can start anywhere else. And any affirmation which begins there will likely honor the Author of that passage.

This does not mean, of course, that all interpretations of Genesis are equal. Understanding and proclaiming the fundamental truth of a passage is one thing. Correctly understanding more detailed meanings of its teaching may be quite different, and it is in the understandings of these meanings that our disagreements will arise. But if we always keep the fundamental truth uppermost in our thoughts and in our lives, our seeking to understand can and will be gracious and loving. Then it will fulfill what God, our *Creator* God, requires of his people in the ninth commandment.

So how should Christians who believe they do know how God "did it" express their disagreement with other Christians who think God did it in a different way? Several further points might assist all of us in expressing such disagreements in ways that fulfill the requirements of the ninth commandment.

Securing Slippery Slopes

For Christians who are inclined to support some form of the theory of evolution, securing their possible slippery slope involves several things.

First is making clear that their understanding of evolution does not negate people's moral accountability to God. That is, of course, one of the perceived dangers of any evolutionary theory: that the theory inevitably leads to the notion that human beings are nothing more than advanced animals. Therefore, they can be no more expected to care about God's Ten Commandments than a household pet does. In other words, does the evolutionary theory allow for any *qualitative* difference between human beings and any of the earlier life forms out of which human beings evolved? If it does, securing this slippery slope requires making it clear that it does and, of equal importance, *how* and *why* it does.

Second, every evolutionary theory with which I am familiar requires reading Genesis 1 through 3 in something other than a literal way. So why does such a reading not inevitably lead to reading the gospel accounts of Christ's death and resurrection in a similar way? I certainly am not accusing everyone who believes a variation of evolutionary theory of interpreting Christ's resurrection as symbolically as they must interpret the word *day* (Hebrew *yom*) in Genesis. But I am arguing that proponents of an evolutionary theory who do not interpret *Christ*

raised from the dead as a purely symbolic statement need to make
that clear. And they need to give some explanation for why they
see this phrase as more literal than the Hebrew word *yom*.

My third and final suggestion to the proponent of any
evolutionary theory is to secure the potentially slippery slope
that has to do with the identity of Adam. Some Christian
proponents of evolutionary theory see Adam as a single individual who, with Eve, sinned and thus brought judgment on
the human race. Other Christian proponents of evolutionary
theory believe and teach that there was no such individual and
that the Hebrew word translated "Adam" can mean simply
"mankind." If the latter position is taken, securing the slippery
slope mandates some kind of explanation of how that position
fits with Paul's argument in Romans 5 affirming a parallel
between the first man Adam and the second man Jesus. At
least such a mandate exists if one really wants to avoid the kind
of "doubtful or equivocal expressions" the ninth commandment prohibits.

The Christian who opposes evolutionary theory also has
some slippery slope securing to do. First, many such Christians often argue that nothing outside the Bible should ever be
used to determine what the Bible can and does say. This may
seem like a valid position, but the Christian espousing such a
view must then make it clear how we know what the words
of Scripture mean if we cannot look outside the Bible to determine their meaning. Even if one says that the Holy Spirit gave
the specific words to the human author of Genesis, how did
the original readers of Genesis know what *yom* meant if they
did not have language outside the Bible which determined
that meaning? How would translators know to translate *yom*
as "day" without some reference to material outside Scripture? For those who reject evolution because of their fear that
it allows external sources such as evolutionary science to determine what the Bible says, securing the slippery slope means

addressing that kind of difficulty in some way. And, of course, that principle applies to any opposition to the use of sources outside the Bible to help us understand the Bible.

Second, Christians who oppose the theory of evolution often tend to be selective in those aspects of secular science they accept and those they reject. Almost all Christians, whatever their position on evolution, clearly trust science when crossing the George Washington Bridge, when taking a flight to London, or when seeking medical assistance for severe chest pain—as well they should! As they argue against the theory of evolution, Christians who don't trust secular science about evolution need to show how they secure the slippery slope so that their attitude still means that they may cross that bridge, take that flight, or consult that physician. In other words, what exactly is it about evolutionary science that leads to its rejection while other types of science seem worthy of trust?

None of this should be interpreted as a statement either for or against the theory of evolution. I am addressing solely the question of how Christians who disagree about this matter should talk as they express their disagreement. The possibility of slippery slopes cannot be wished away.

What Do You Really Want?[14]

One final point needs to be made with respect to disagreements about evolution. The huge range of positions within both evolution camps demands that we be very sure exactly what our opponents are advocating before we speak about what we believe to be their error. In some ways, this may seem like the old problem of labels. But it is more than that. For example, those who hold to theistic evolution and those who hold to evolutionary creationism genuinely support the idea of some kind of evolution. But they differ strongly on what form that evolution took. Likewise, those who hold to young earth creationism and those who hold to old earth creationism agree in their emphasis on the creative work of God. But they differ strongly on the length of time God took in creating. And two evangelical Christian intellectual giants like Francis Collins and John Lennox, while profoundly respecting each other, don't hesitate to make public (in a very gracious way) their disagreements over matters relating to evolution while still both maintaining a vigorous rejection of atheistic evolutionary theory.[15]

The bottom line: before we express disagreement with someone who seems to support or someone who seems to oppose evolution, we must be sure of what that person is really saying. This means the first sentences out of our mouths when dealing with this subject must be a question, not a declaration. Asking questions is essential to bearing true witness.

And toward the conclusion of any discussion about evolution, remember: "If, in the end, I cannot agree with you on this subject, what would you most like to see from me and others who take my position?"

WOMEN IN MINISTRY LEADERSHIP

As I write this, one of the most vigorous controversies roiling the evangelical church is which (if any) roles women may play in church leadership positions, and the degree to which women must remain subordinate to men in those positions.

Let's approach this issue from a slightly different direction. The publisher of the English Standard Version of the Bible recently released an updated translation in which the translators have changed their wording of Genesis 3:16, which is part of the curse on the woman after she sins. The old translation read, "Your desire shall be for your husband, and he shall rule over you," and the new one is, "Your desire shall be contrary to your husband, but he shall rule over you." Reactions to this change have tended to depend on what views people already have about women in ministry leadership. Complementarians (who emphasize different roles for men and women) seem to support the new translation of that verse, while egalitarians (who emphasize similar roles for men and women) seem to be opposed. It seems that views about this issue are so strong they even drive how we think Scripture should be translated.

How amazing are the dimensions of the women-in-ministry question! How often have we heard that, if a church ordains women to all offices for which men can be ordained (one act of full recognition of women in ministry), the church is giving a clear indication that they are liberal. And breaking away from that church is not only acceptable, it is required![16] Alternatively, how often have we heard that those churches which do not approve the ordination of women to all offices for which men can be ordained exemplify the worst attributes of misogynist theologizing and should be shunned as narrow-minded and fundamentalist?[17]

My own convictions focus on two separate issues which, in my reading of Scripture, seem to be somewhat in tension with each other, much as the issues of divine sovereignty and human responsibility seem to be in tension with each other. Please note my use of the words seem to be. Our Lord does not contradict himself. But he is far above us, and sometimes it can be hard to see exactly how the tensions in Scripture all hold together.

God did say to both Adam and Eve, "Be fruitful and increase in number; fill the earth and subdue it. Rule over the fish in the sea and the birds in the sky and over every living creature that moves on the ground" (Genesis 1:28). And God uses women in the New Testament in accomplishing his kingdom ends (see Matthew 28:5–8; Acts 9:36; 16:14–15).

At the same time, whichever rendering one takes of Genesis 3:16, God indicates that something more than pure biology characterizes the relationship between men and women. Further, in 1 Corinthians 14:34–35 and 1 Timothy 2:8–15, some ministry restrictions are placed specifically on women.

Therefore, my convictions about this issue involve obedience to both of these strands of biblical teaching. In *both* our personal lives and in our preaching or teaching, we must vigorously affirm both that women are responsible to carry out kingdom responsibilities just like men and must be given opportunities to do so and that there are some biblical statements about how ministry is to be carried out which suggest differences between men and women. How these two statements are harmonized in practice may differ from culture to culture, or denomination to denomination. But neither may be ignored if we are going to live in full obedience to God's Word.

In addition to the apparent tension between two strands of biblical teaching about the role of women in the ministry of the church, I must admit that I have an increasing sense that the definition of ordination, especially as the word is often used in Western contexts, needs much greater clarification. The Greek words translated "ordain" or "ordained" are used in very different ways in different places in the New Testament. In addition to "ordain," those words may be translated as "decided on," "determined by," "appointed by," "decreed by," or "elected."

For example, the Greek word *poieo* in Mark 3:14 is translated "ordained" in the King James Version: "And he *ordained* twelve, that they should be with him, and that he might send them forth to preach." But in Matthew 23:15, the KJV renders the same word as "made" and "make": "Woe unto you, scribes and Pharisees, hypocrites! for ye compass sea and land to *make* one proselyte, and when he is *made*, ye make him twofold more the child of hell than yourselves." The NIV translates that same word as "appointed" in Mark 3:14 and "win" and "make" in Matthew 23:15.

I remember vividly a conversation I had with two Ugandan women at a conference in Jerusalem in 2018. I made a comment about the fact that, in the USA, the ordination of women was an issue over which many evangelical denominations had split. The Ugandans were incredulous. "How in the world does the work of the church get done if you don't use women preachers?" They then went on to press me, graciously but firmly, about the biblical basis for the whole notion of ordination. Along with a similar conversation I had with some evangelical Brazilians, this Jerusalem experience has led me personally to the conclusion that the whole idea of ordination seems to need a great deal more work. And that work must invite and carefully consider input from biblical scholars in what we call the Majority World. But even then, we will continue to be faced with disagreements among Christians on the appropriate roles women may and should play in Christian ministry. And that means we need to think carefully about how we talk about those with whom we disagree on this most important subject—important because it involves at least half the church.

Stay on Point and Cast No Aspersions

First, of course, we forswear the use of labels when describing a particular person. The words *complementarian* and *egalitarian* need, at the very least, significant explanation when applied to anyone, including ourselves. I have never met a complementarian who did not believe that men and women are equal before God. And I have never met an egalitarian who does not believe that the Bible's description of the creation of Eve means that men and women are intended by God to complement each other. Of course, the terms do denote some significant differences between the positions. But the more I genuinely want to understand that person with whom I am disagreeing, and that person wants to understand me, the more something beyond labels will be required.

Beyond those specific and oft-used terms, I recommend that those who favor the full utilization of women's gifts with few if any restrictions avoid the following labels when speaking about those with whom they disagree on this subject: *misogynist*, *narrow-minded*, *sexist/sexism*, *chauvinist*, and *unbiblical*. Conversely, I recommend that those who believe the Bible does place significant restrictions on the way in which women should utilize their gifts in the church avoid the following labels when speaking about those who disagree with them: *liberal*, *neo-orthodox*, *feminist*, *modernist*, and *unbiblical*.

Of course, conversations with others about this subject must begin with Scripture itself and must include the specific passages mentioned above. Other legitimate Bible-based discussion topics would include the following:

- How exactly do we understand the significance of the cultural contexts of passages like Genesis 1:28 and 3:16, 1 Corinthians 14, and 1 Timothy 2? To what degree, if at all, should we consider the cultural norms of the societies that first received those writings?

- Are there any other passages in either the Old or the New Testament where evangelical theology generally recognizes the legitimacy of such cultural hermeneutics? If there are, what are those passages? How are they similar to or different from the passages which address the relationships of men and women?

- What, if anything, are we meant to learn from the fact that some women filled leadership roles in both the Old and New Testaments? What, if anything, does it mean that women were not chosen as priests in the Old Testament or as disciples of Jesus in the New Testament? What kinds of broad hermeneutical principles are we able and willing to draw from the way we answer the preceding two questions?

- Does the understanding of ordination that is dominant in the American evangelical church have solid biblical warrant? What exactly is that warrant? To what degree, if at all, should we seek the wisdom of the non-Westernized Majority World church in dealing with the ordination question?

- American evangelicals differ vigorously on issues like baptism. Yet those differences don't seem to produce the level of suspicion and dissension that the issue of women in ministry produces. Why might this be so?

Securing Slippery Slopes

Then there is the matter of securing the slippery slopes. Discussions of women in ministry leadership usually contain a plethora of those nasty slopes, the most important of which emerge directly out of the five discussion topics suggested above.

For example, those who affirm that cultural contexts should, perhaps *always*, be considered in our interpretation of biblical texts must make clear the limitations of that if they want to preserve any sense of the special character of Scripture. Without setting clear and specific limitations, even Jesus might become merely an adaptation of such pagan figures as Osiris, Dionysus, Adonis, Attis, and Mithras. To put it another way, those who want to use cultural contexts to interpret some Scripture must demonstrate why and where Dan Brown is wrong when he suggests, in *The DaVinci Code*, that "nothing in Christianity is original."[18]

On the other side, those who assert that cultural contexts should not be used in the interpretation of biblical texts must make clear how they would respond to what was said about the very meaning of the words of Scripture. How do we even know the meaning of the Greek words in 1 Corinthians 14 and 1 Timothy 2 if we do not consider their cultural context?

In fact, when any discussion of women in ministry leadership is held between professing Christians, both sides seem to agree that some aspects of extra-biblical culture may be used to interpret Scripture. But both sides equally insist that, in other ways, the Bible stands outside human culture and, in fact, ultimately judges all cultures. So both sides need to secure the slippery slope to make clear the limits—and the reason for the specific limits—of the use of extra-biblical culture to interpret passages in the Bible.

In addition, those who read 1 Timothy 2:12 ("I do not permit a woman to teach or to assume authority over a man; she must be quiet") to prohibit women from serving as preachers must show how they guard their reading of this passage against the slippery slope that slides into prohibiting any female from ever teaching a male anything. Is this prohibition related just to church situations? Why? How do we know? Does it apply to situations which are clearly religious but not under the control of any specific church? And are there any age restrictions on the passage? May a widow teach her college-bound son how to open a checking account? We tend to disregard such extreme questions. But making clear where the limitation comes in this passage helps both in our discussions with those who disagree with us and in our own living consistently under the authority of that passage.

Similarly, those who interpret 1 Timothy 2:12 and other such passages as not prohibiting women from preaching or from other positions of authority need to indicate where the equality of men and women stops, if it stops at all. Should women and men serve equally in military combat situations? Should men and women have equal maternity/paternity leave? Should all athletic activities be open to everyone, regardless of gender? Harvard recently determined that it would punish any student who joins a single-gender organization.[19] Is this kind of action the inevitable result of the equality slippery slope? If not, how would one secure the slope so that such policies are not required? Again, we tend to disregard such extreme questions. But making clear what boundaries there are to the equality of the sexes greatly helps in our discussions with those who disagree with us and in our own living consistently under the authority of that passage.

For clearly evangelical but significantly different perspectives on this difficult issue, I recommend *Man and Woman: One in Christ* by Philip Barton Payne and *Different by Design: God's Blueprint for Men and Women* by Carrie Sandom.[20] These books demonstrate how evangelicals who take equally high views of Scripture can come to totally different positions on the question of women in ministry leadership. We should certainly avoid violating the ninth commandment by the way in which we talk about any professing Christian who takes either of these positions.

What Do You Really Want?

And, of course, toward the conclusion of any discussion about women in ministry leadership, remember: "If, in the end, I cannot come to agree with you on this subject, what would you most like to see from me and others who take my position?"

SOCIAL JUSTICE

"Those who focus their preaching and teaching on things like poverty and racial discrimination and the plight of refugees are unquestionably liberals and may not even be a Christians. The important issues are spiritual. And that's where our attention must be centered. Just read the book of Romans!"

"No, as a matter of fact, those who do not address the plight of the poor and the marginalized and the hurting obviously have not read the Bible and are not worthy of the name *Christian*. Just look at how much time Jesus spends dealing with the poor and the weak and the oppressed!"

These are both extreme and fictional statements. But I have heard similar statements over and over—all coming from those whom I regard as my brothers and sisters in Christ. The dividing line often seems to come between those who emphasize what Christians must believe and those who emphasize what we should do.

In this discussion, the phrase *social justice* means the kinds of issues listed in Isaiah 58:6–7 and mentioned by Jesus in his Parable of the Sheep the Goats in Matthew 25:31–46, which are concerns like freedom for the oppressed, food for the hungry, and shelter for strangers. A deep divide exists on this subject. When a group of evangelical leaders led by well-known pastor John MacArthur recently released the *Dallas Statement on Social Justice and the Gospel*, it seemed to generate as much opposition as agreement, with *Christianity Today* declaring, "Christians are Talking Past Each Other Once Again."[21]

Most evangelicals on both sides of this issue profess and demonstrate a profound concern for the teachings of Scripture. Often, when I have engaged with representatives of either side, I have found myself instructed in biblical perspectives and in the total scope of what our gracious Lord desires all of his people to be and to do. This certainly may be a result of how terribly far I am from complete "right understanding" and full "evangelical obedience," but I suspect that we all might benefit from more of both of these characteristics of Christian discipleship. I suggest, therefore, that we should assume that we can learn from discussions about social justice. Amazingly, it seems to me that when we make this assumption, it is proven correct. And when we make the opposite assumption, that also is proven correct.

My position on this subject is that *what we believe and what we do are equally important*. Neither is more important than the other. Neither correct belief nor correct behavior earns a heavenly reward. God gives to his people any graces which he then blesses: "Every good and perfect gift is from above, coming down from the Father of the heavenly lights, who does not change like shifting shadows" (James 1:17). God gets the credit for anything we do that is good. This also should be our motive for both our faith and our actions: we believe and trust in him because he deserves our belief and trust. Anyone who makes either theology or obedience more important than the other is failing to see that both are equally the means by which our chief end can be achieved—that of glorifying God and enjoying him forever.

Of course, there are some—probably many—who disagree with my position. So how should I talk about them and how should they talk about me? By now, the drill should be clear. And it starts with avoiding labels because they likely lie.

Stay on Point and Cast No Aspersions

What have you heard about those evangelicals who strongly argue that doctrine matters and that precise distinctions among competing theologies must be made if we are to be true to Scripture? I have heard that such individuals are "out of touch," that they have reduced the gospel to a bunch of irrelevant abstractions, and that they are ignoring where Jesus seems to have placed the emphasis in his own life and ministry. I have heard them called unloving and uncaring.

What have you heard about Christians who place a heavy emphasis on social justice and who spend significant time discussing our obligations to the poor and the oppressed? What have you read about those Christians who insist that our first response to refugees must be to do all that we can to welcome them and to care for them and to provide for them? I have heard that those Christians are liberals, that they have "bought into the social gospel," that they see Christianity as a kind of sanctified welfare state.

Unfortunately, some of us may be described in exactly these ways. I see in my own life patterns of belief and behavior which might legitimately be called some of these things. No one has less right to claim full sanctification than me. But perhaps a few of my readers can also feel the shoe fitting fairly well. Perhaps we all struggle with things we shouldn't do, or things we fail to do. My point has never been that those on one side of any of the issues I have addressed are universally more (or less) righteous than those on the other side. *All* have sinned and fall short of the glory of God.

Labelling a serious and precise Christian theologian "unloving" bears false witness. Labelling a Christian social activist as "liberal" bears false witness.

In fact, most of those with whom we disagree on this particular subject simply appear to us to have over-emphasized one or the other aspect of the "faith vs. works" apparent dichotomy. Please note the critically important word apparent. No dichotomy actually exists in Scripture. The Bible mandates both faith and full obedience; we don't get to pick one or the other. But we often sense, from divine guidance or perhaps for some less sanctified reason, that we are personally called to focus our kingdom energies on either "perfecting the faith" or "loving our neighbor." And we do well to heed that call. However, when we do, we may feel inclined to question a fellow Christian who senses a call to focus on the other type of activity. Therefore, good conversation with or about someone whose call seems to be different from our own should start with a request: "Help me to see from Scripture why you think what you are doing honors the Lord." Or, via social media:

"Would my Facebook friends help me to see from Scripture how X honors the Lord?"

Such requests, if made genuinely and not as veiled accusations, will always produce good results—precisely because they take both parties straight to the Bible. And, sure enough, the Bible teaches both. For example, it's hard to ignore the need to love our neighbor if we've read the passage from Isaiah 58 mentioned earlier.

> "Is not this the kind of fasting I have chosen:
> to loose the chains of injustice
>   and untie the cords of the yoke,
> to set the oppressed free
>   and break every yoke?
> Is it not to share your food with the hungry
>   and to provide the poor wanderer with shelter—
> when you see the naked, to clothe them,
>   and not to turn away from your own flesh and
> blood?
>
> "Then your light will break forth like the dawn,
>   and your healing will quickly appear;
> then your righteousness will go before you,
>   and the glory of the Lord will be your rear guard.
> Then you will call, and the Lord will answer;
>   you will cry for help, and he will say: Here am I.
>
> "If you do away with the yoke of oppression,
>   with the pointing finger and malicious talk,
> and if you spend yourselves in behalf of the hungry
>   and satisfy the needs of the oppressed,
> then your light will rise in the darkness,
>   and your night will become like the noonday."
> (Isaiah 58:6–10)

It's equally hard to ignore the need for right theology, and for perfecting the faith, if we've read Peter's confession that Jesus is the Christ.

> When Jesus came to the region of Caesarea Philippi, he asked his disciples, "Who do people say the Son of Man is?" They replied, "Some say John the Baptist; others say Elijah; and still others, Jeremiah or one of the prophets."
>
> "But what about you?" he asked. "Who do you say I am?"
>
> Simon Peter answered, "You are the Messiah, the Son of the living God."
>
> Jesus replied, "Blessed are you, Simon son of Jonah, for this was not revealed to you by flesh and blood, but by my Father in heaven. And I tell you that you are Peter, and on this rock I will build my church, and the gates of Hades will not overcome it. I will give you the keys of the kingdom of heaven; whatever you bind on earth will be bound in heaven, and whatever you loose on earth will be loosed in heaven." (Matthew 16:13–19)

Scripture clearly teaches both—perfecting the faith and loving our neighbor—and we do well to heed that total teaching, even if our personal calling is to focus primarily on one or the other.

Securing Slippery Slopes

The next step must be to secure the slippery slope. Those whose Christian calling involves primarily activities which might fall under the rubric of "loving my neighbor" must regularly and clearly demonstrate, in word and deed, that the doctrinal teachings of Scripture are not irrelevant to them and their calling. Indeed, such Christians should make it abundantly clear that they have been propelled into their form of service by God speaking through his authoritative Word. In some of their activities, Christians might very well and properly work alongside those who reject Christianity. No problem, unless the Christians intentionally choose to avoid ever making it clear that they are working in Jesus's name. When the hungry are fed, Jesus is honored. But if we are afraid of the response we might get if we mention him directly as the reason for our work, he surely is not honored.

Similarly, when "loving" Christians speak or write about their calling, they must be careful to make certain that the broader theological context of their calling cannot be missed. They must not leave any doubt where they stand theologically because, if they do, they will be communicating equivocally. Because our actions speak, there must be no doubtfulness in those actions. Those who disagree with us about the importance of living lives which embody social justice are not responsible to ferret out where we stand theologically. It must be clear that we do not reduce the gospel to good works, so clear that the Lord's words to Habakkuk become true in us: "And the Lord answered me, 'Write the vision; make it plain on tablets, *so he may run who reads it*'" (Habakkuk 2:2 ESV, *emphasis added*). Even if champion sprinter Usain Bolt runs past us while we are serving food to a homeless person, he should be able to see Jesus's face in what we are doing. That will secure the slippery slope.

Those whose calling seems to focus primarily on "perfecting the faith" have similar responsibilities. For them, the slippery slope does not lead to a social gospel but to precisionist irrelevancy. How often Scripture addresses this slippery slope!

Hearing that Jesus had silenced the Sadducees, the Pharisees got together. One of them, an expert in the law, tested him with this question: "Teacher, which is the greatest commandment in the Law?" Jesus replied: "'Love the Lord your God with all your heart and with all your soul and with all your mind.' This is the first and greatest commandment. And the second is like it: 'Love your neighbor as yourself.' All the Law and the Prophets hang on these two commandments." (Matthew 22:34–40)

"Woe to you, teachers of the law and Pharisees, you hypocrites! You give a tenth of your spices—mint, dill and cumin. But you have neglected the more important matters of the law—justice, mercy and faithfulness. You should have practiced the latter, without neglecting the former. You blind guides! You strain out a gnat but swallow a camel." (Matthew 23:23–24)

The church desperately needs those who will "perfect the faith." Especially in early twenty-first century Western culture, the truths of Scripture must be affirmed and made abundantly clear. The more biblical our theological affirmations, the more honor is brought to Jesus. But when we ignore those around us who are hurting or when we unnecessarily hurt others—even as part of our attempt to perfect the faith—he surely is not honored.

When "faith perfecting" Christians speak or write about their calling, they must be careful to make certain that the loving dimensions of that calling cannot be missed. They must leave no doubt by how they speak and act that they believe Isaiah 58 is as inerrant as any other passage of Scripture. Otherwise, they will be communicating equivocally.

Those who disagree with us are not responsible to ferret out whether we love our neighbors. It must be so clear that we do not reduce the gospel to correct theology that, again, he who runs may read it.

What Do You Really Want?

And, of course, at or toward the conclusion of any discussion about making abundantly clear the importance of both loving our neighbor and perfecting the faith, consider these as your closing words: "If, in the end, I cannot come to agree with you on this subject, what would you most like to see from me and others who take my position?"

SAME-SEX MARRIAGE

Possibly the most hotly debated current subject among serious Christians around the world is the issue of same-sex marriage. Many religious groups which have agreed to allow disagreement among their members about most of the issues mentioned above have made this a point on which agreement is required. And the language used by disagreeing parties when discussing this matter can be especially inflammatory.

My position? I believe Scripture teaches that the blessings of sexual activity are to be found exclusively in heterosexual, monogamous, life-long relationships. Jesus's teaching in Matthew 19:1–12 and Mark 10:1–12 gives the basis for this. As part of his explanation of marriage, Jesus taught, "At the beginning the Creator 'made them male and female,' and said, 'For this reason a man will leave his father and mother and be united to his wife, and the two will become one flesh'? So they are no longer two, but one flesh. Therefore what God has joined together, let no one separate" (Matthew 19:4–6). Jesus also provides the only biblical exception to this, and this exception has to do solely with when it is permissible to end a monogamous, heterosexual marriage: "I tell you that anyone who divorces his wife, except for sexual immorality, and marries another woman commits adultery" (v. 9).

I further believe that God has, in his Word, commanded that we have no sexual activity outside monogamous, life-long, heterosexual relationships. Many books provide a full discussion of this position and many provide extensive discussions of other perspectives on this matter. My intention here is not to try to defend my position, and I recognize that I could be wrong. But even if I am, that would not necessarily negate my essential points about how to discuss same-sex marriage.

Stay on Point and Cast No Aspersions

Moving to that topic, what are the labels we ought to avoid as we express our concerns about same-sex marriage? Of course, the entire spectrum of issues in what is commonly known as LBGTQ presents matters for discussion. But I will focus on the "G" and the "L" components and will use the phrase same-sex marriage.

A few labels come easily and quickly to mind. Those who share the heterosexual marriage position I have just described must, at the very least, avoid these labels when speaking to or about those who disagree with them: *degenerate, promiscuous, unregenerate, sex-obsessed, unfaithful,* and other similar terms. Of course, some who support same-sex marriage may be some of these things. But so may be some who do not support same-sex marriage!

In fact, my first version of this chapter contained labels and terms which I have since learned are inappropriate and possibly offensive. Among those terms are *gay lifestyle* and *homosexual/gay agenda*. My instruction came from the report of a study committee of the Christian Reformed Church in North America. The following is from that report:

> In our listening sessions, we were troubled by the repeated occurrence of certain terms. Use of these is less than truthful, and certainly not gracious. These terms were, in most cases, being used by pastors and church leaders. Two terms that should be avoided are:

Gay lifestyle—this term is sometimes used to explain one's opposition to all same-sex relationships. Saying "I'm opposed to the gay lifestyle" evokes stereotypes of gay bars, promiscuous behavior, surreptitious rendez-vous, and a flagrant counterculture of gay socializa-tion—and then applies this stereotype to all same-sex oriented relationships. There is no such thing as "the gay lifestyle," just as there is no "heterosexual lifestyle." There are simply ways people live. It is highly offensive to same-sex oriented persons when opposition to "the gay lifestyle" is invoked.

Homosexual/gay agenda—this term is problematic as well and should be avoided by those in the Christian church. It uses negative associations with the word agenda to explain changes within society and to insinu-ate a coordinated conspiracy to improperly advance the interests of one group over against another. Most social changes are of complex origin. Christians would do best to avoid the language of insinuation and conspiracy. In-stead we should speak in terms that resonate with the Christian faith's language of justice, fairness, and flour-ishing.[22]

Because there are other, less offensive ways to communicate our concerns, there seems to be no reason to use the phrases *gay lifestyle* and *homosexual/gay agenda*. As I continued to try to learn as I wrote, I removed the terms. And I suspect that few people will even be able to tell where they originally appeared. This is part of what it means to stay on point and cast no asper-sions.

But what about professed Christians who support same-sex marriage? What labels should they avoid? When speaking of other professed Christians, they should certainly avoid *homophobic, hateful, narrow-minded, bigoted, stupid, unenlightened*, and other such terms. Of course, some of those who oppose same-sex marriage may actually be some of these things. But so may be some who support same-sex marriages. If one professed Christian thinks another professed Christian is hateful, he or she should address that issue in a way which does not rely on offensive labels.

Another part of the process of staying on point and casting no aspersions involves refraining from labelling this (or any other) specific activity as the unforgivable sin. This is certainly a complex issue and there is no way that I would ever feel competent to provide an exhaustive list of all possible sins ranked in the order of their severity. What shapes my thought most in this regard is what Jonathan Edwards says about the very nature of sin in his *Treatise on Original Sin*. Edwards points out that, as much as the church and individual Christians may focus on sins of commission, the biblical emphasis on sins of omission must never be forgotten.

The various catechisms I cited in chapter 2 seem to understand this. One simply has to look at what the *Westminster Larger Catechism* affirms to be the positive duties required in each of the commandments. About the first commandment, Westminster says this:

> The duties required in the first commandment are, the knowing and acknowledging of God to be the only true God, and our God; and to worship and glorify him accordingly, by thinking, meditating, remembering, highly esteeming, honoring, adoring, choosing, loving, desiring, fearing of him; believing him; trusting, hoping, delighting, rejoicing in him; being zealous for him; calling upon him, giving all praise and thanks, and yielding all obedience and submission to him with the whole man; being careful in all things to please him, and sorrowful when in anything he is offended; and

walking humbly with him. (*Westminster Larger Catechism*, question 104)

In other words, we have broken this first commandment given by God whenever we do not do all of these things. And Jesus reinforces this idea in response to a question about the greatest commandment: "Jesus replied: 'Love the Lord your God with all your heart and with all your soul and with all your mind.' This is the first and greatest commandment. And the second is like it: 'Love your neighbor as yourself.' All the Law and the Prophets hang on these two commandments" (Matthew 22:37–40).

Note the repetition of the word *all*. Of course, loving God with all my heart, soul, and mind surely involves not doing what God prohibits. But it also involves all of the things cited by the catechism. Jonathan Edwards summarizes this teaching as follows: "Whoever withholds more of that love or respect from God, which his law requires, than he affords, has more sin than righteousness."[23] And Edwards drives the point home with this incredible example:

> Therefore how absurd must it be for Christians to object, against the depravity of man's nature, a greater number of innocent and kind actions, than of crimes; and to talk of a prevailing innocence, good nature, industry, and cheerfulness of the greater part of mankind! Infinitely more absurd, than it would be to insist, that the domestic of a prince was not a bad servant, because though sometimes he contemned and affronted his master to a great degree, yet he did not spit in his master's face so often as he performed acts of service. More absurd, than it would be to affirm, that his spouse was a good wife to him, because, although she committed adultery, and that with the slaves and scoundrels sometimes, yet she did not do this so often as she did the duties of a wife.

These notions would be absurd, because the crimes are too heinous to be atoned for, by many honest actions of the servant or spouse of the prince; there being a vast disproportion between the merit of the one, and the ill desert of the other: but infinitely less, than that between the demerit of our offenses against God, and the value of our acts of obedience.[24]

The bottom line? That each of us should avoid labeling what we see as the sins of others as being somehow greater than our own sins. *Any* sin requires repentance. And "there's power in the blood" to cleanse *every* sin. To be specific, we should seek, by the power of God's Spirit, to make sure that we never spit in our Master's face by violating the ninth commandment when we talk to or about those with whom we disagree about same-sex marriage.

Securing Slippery Slopes

As was the case with the other specific issues discussed above, both sides in any discussion of same-sex marriage must remain open to considering seriously what someone else might see as the slippery slope of the argument.

From the one side, those who believe that Scripture prohibits same-sex marriage need to think carefully about all of the commands of Scripture. They must be prepared to discuss whether what they see as the Bible's prohibition of homosexuality carries more spiritual weight than the many commands about loving one's neighbor and care for the poor and avoiding damage to the good name of one's neighbor. Often, those who are outspoken in support of the position which I hold seem to pay significantly less attention to a wide variety of other patterns of conduct on which the Bible places greater emphasis. If anything, for example, Jesus speaks much more directly and clearly about divorce than he does about homosexuality. Why exactly should churches consider homosexual activity more heinous than other sins of commission or, indeed, more heinous than sins of omission? There may be good biblical reasons for this, but securing the slippery slope in this discussion requires that those reasons be stated clearly.

From the opposite side, those who believe that the Bible does not prohibit same-sex marriage need to be prepared to discuss what limits, if any, the Bible does place on human sexual activity. Polygamy is just one of the many slippery slopes that needs securing by advocates for this position. In today's hook-up culture, many individuals seem to think that there are no restrictions on sexual expression. If the relatively narrow limits proposed by those who oppose homosexual activity are not binding on Christians, what limits are? There may be good biblical support for much greater sexual freedom but, if there is, securing this particular slippery slope requires that such evidence be stated clearly.

What Do You Really Want?

Even after extended gracious discussion, disagreements over the precise teaching of Scripture likely will remain. How then to proceed? Keep talking. Keep loving. Continue avoiding labels. Continue staying on subject. Continue desiring more than anything else that the other party to the discussion will ultimately come to believe and act in the way which maximizes the honor brought to Jesus and will therefore experience great blessing from the Lord. In other words, whatever you do, don't be a Jonah!

To help with this extended and sometimes painful process, give thought to the ways in which you might, without compromising your beliefs, speak and act in ways that communicate to the other party that your love and care for them remains undiminished and that you want to love them just as Jesus loves you. Seek specific concerns on which you can genuinely agree and, with honesty and enthusiasm, show your support for these concerns. Even though I oppose same-sex marriage, I supported the executive action President Obama took in 2010 to assure that all hospitals that participate in Medicare and Medicaid allow patients to designate who may visit them in the hospital. Perhaps others who share my position cannot agree with that. But at least try to find common ground.[25]

Another point on this topic applies mainly, though not exclusively, to those Christians who share my views about same-sex marriage. We are basically asking those of the opposite view not to support or act on something that genuinely seems right to them. Of course, this is often the case with biblical directives or prohibitions, but I sense that this is especially true with respect to matters relating to same-sex attraction and marriage. My plea to all who share my position is a simple one: take care to understand the profundity of what we are asking of those whom we see as our opponents on this issue. Take the time to read a book like *Washed and Waiting* by Wesley Hill.[26] Get a sense of what it may cost some people if they do come to agree with the position we are espousing. This suggestion in no way mitigates the need for us to speak truth as we understand the truth. But it may help us to be even more caring and careful with the words we use. And caring, careful words always honor Jesus.

An excellent example of how to talk to others, even firmly, about disagreements regarding same-sex marriage is the online article by Scott Sauls, "Can Christians and the LBGTQ Community Be Friends."[27] His positive answer to the question has, as unfortunately might be expected, provoked significant and sharply negative reaction in the blogosphere, with one article I read labelling it "toxic." Disagreement can and should be expressed without the use of such labels.

Finally, any expression of disagreement between professing Christians on this subject should conclude with the question, "If, after all of our discussion, I cannot come to agree with you on this subject, what would you most like to see from me and others who take my position?"

ACCUSATIONS OF SEXUAL WRONGDOING

While there is surely no disagreement among Christians about the wrongness of sexual harassment, abuse, or consensual sexual sin, there just as surely is disagreement about whether and how to make public comment about such accusations. Sadly, sexual impropriety in evangelical Christian communities is real, and it is essential that it be addressed. Those who have been harassed or abused need the support of their spiritual family, the Christian community. Providing that support is an essential mark of the Christian church, the body of Christ. Similarly, those involved in sexual sin need the caring, loving discipline of that body. Jonahs should stay away.

As in the rest of this book, my point here has to do exclusively with public statements, on social media or elsewhere. In order to appropriately protect the good names of our Christian brothers and sisters and of the Savior they profess, we should avoid naming individuals or even suggesting names in any public forum unless we have direct, firsthand knowledge of the specific situations and unless we are absolutely certain that we know *all* the facts. It is critically important to remember that I am here discussing "public" statements on platforms such as Facebook. My cautions do not apply to the reporting of sexual abuse (confirmed or suspected) to appropriate legal authorities. As with any other suspected crimes, our duties as Christian citizens require us to inform the police of our suspicions. But the duties I have been outlining elsewhere in this book prohibit our then announcing publicly what we have reported to the authorities.

Even if we do have firsthand knowledge of all the facts, we should speak in public only when it is genuinely necessary for us do so to provide support or discipline. To be sure that we are correct about such necessity, consulting the church(es) of the individual(s) involved before making any public statements is appropriate. More work? Probably so! More likely obedience to the total teaching of Scripture? Absolutely yes!!

Providentially, a recent example of how to publicly address matters relating to accusations of sexual harassment, abuse, or consensual sexual sin has been provided. It suggests a practice that should be followed whenever public statements are made about any issue on which there is disagreement among Christians. Andy Crouch at *Christianity Today International* wrote a blog post to tell of a bad week: in three separate cases, powerful Christian leaders he knew were confronted with allegations of sexual misconduct. Here is what Crouch wrote about these three leaders:

> I am not naming them here. If you are in their sphere of influence, you've already had the wind knocked out of you by the week's revelations, and there is no need to re-double the trauma. If you are not, then the desire to know their names, though understandable and human, is a prurience I will not indulge. And while I pray that such a tragic trifecta will not happen often in a single week, the truth is that I could have written this essay many times in the past few decades, and will have occasion to do so many times in the future. The names are actually not that important for my purposes—it is the system in which not just they, but we, are so deeply complicit.[28]

As the post states, the desire to know and to name names is understandable and human. But such a desire may simply be an example of prurience, an unhealthy interest in sex.

When I raised this kind of concern with a Facebook friend, he responded that he was naming names in the interest of transparency. Transparency is good. More transparency would surely be helpful in the evangelical Christian community. But transparency is good and helpful only when I am being transparent about *my own weaknesses and sin*. Transparency about someone else's possible weaknesses and sin, especially his or her possible sexual weaknesses and sin, may be simple prurience.

We also need to remember to avoid blanket assertions about groups. I probably violate the intent of the ninth commandment if I seek to make transparent the sins of "evangelicals," even if I self-identify as an evangelical. This is why, if you read his lengthy post, you will find that Crouch spends most of his time being transparent about his own personal temptations and his own personal attempts to secure the slippery slope of his own nature. This is the kind of transparency we need. This is the kind of transparency which best addresses sin without compromising the good name of our neighbor or of our Savior.

Crouch's post is also a good example of how we should address what we perceive to be the errors in another Christian's theology or behavior. Address the issue. Address it strongly and at length. But keep in mind all that the ninth commandment and the rest of Scripture teach about protecting the names of our Christian neighbors.

CONCLUSION

In conclusion, I would like to cite one more excellent example of how to respond to those with whom we genuinely disagree. This example is from the life and ministry of the Savior whose name we bear. It is often called the Parable of the Prodigal Son, but probably should be given a different title.

The story begins with a disagreement: "Now the tax collectors and sinners were all gathering around to hear Jesus. But the Pharisees and the teachers of the law muttered, 'This man welcomes sinners and eats with them'" (Luke 15:1–2).

Jesus's response to these critics not only shows that a firm and gracious, "true-witness-bearing" response is possible, it also suggests what such a response might look like.

Jesus responds with three parables: the Parable of the Lost Sheep, the Parable of the Lost Coin, and the Parable of the Prodigal (or Lost) Son. Those titles tend to obscure the true brilliance of what Jesus is saying, because the disagreement that leads Jesus to tell them is not about the people gathering around Jesus but about Jesus himself. It is he, not the tax collectors and sinners, at whom the muttering is primarily directed.

This means that in each of the three parables, our focus must be on the three characters who most closely correspond to Jesus. These would be the shepherd who looks for the sheep, the woman who looks for the coin, and the father who watches for his son. Therefore, a better title for Jesus's third story might be, "The Parable of the Running Father." Jesus is asking his critics to see that his conversations with sinners and tax collectors are like the actions of the shepherd, the woman, and the father.

All three stories perfectly reflect the final words of God to Jonah that we looked at earlier: "Should I not have concern for the great city of Nineveh, in which there are more than a hundred and twenty thousand people who cannot tell their right hand from their left—and also many animals?" (Jonah 4:11).

Jesus's response to the muttering Pharisees could be paraphrased, "Should I not have as much concern for these sinners and tax collectors as a shepherd has for his lost sheep, as a woman has for her lost coin, and as a father has for his lost son?" And the subtext of that paraphrase might be, "Should not you also show that same kind of concern?"

One of the most remarkable things about these three parables is that, by telling them, Jesus takes the same loving concern he had for the tax collectors and sinners and extends it to the Pharisees. Jesus knew the hearts of those grumblers. He had the authority to speak strong words of judgment against them, as he did on other occasions. But here he shows that it is possible to respond to error with firm but winsome grace. He speaks in a way designed to move them from error to truth while, at the same time, he protects his good name and defends the sinners who had gathered around him. May God help us to do the same.

SELECTED GUIDELINES FOR BEARING TRUE WITNESS

The items here have been created by groups of evangelical Christians to provide guidance on bearing true witness. I include them to show that there is broad recognition of the problem and the dangers of bearing false witness within the Christian community, and as examples of how this might be addressed in ways that fit the biblical requirements presented in this book. I commend these examples to readers of this book.

Online Resources from the World Reformed Fellowship

The WRF has several documents suggesting ways to prevent sexually-based misconduct and handle accusations about it, including matters relating to how Christian churches and organizations should speak publicly about allegations. These can be found at wrfnet.org, in two articles:

- "Suggestions Regarding Interpersonal Relationships in Christian Churches and Organizations," http://wrfnet.org/articles/2018/08/suggestions-regarding-

interpersonal-relationships-christian-churches-and#.
XAW7OPZFxMs.

- "Corroboration of Accusations of Sexual Misconduct,"
  http://wrfnet.org/articles/2018/11/concerning-
  corroboration-accusations-sexual-misconduct-
  christian-environments#.XAW7hPZFxMs.

Document 1: Some Thoughts on Christian Civility

NOTE: In October of 2017, the World Reformed
Fellowship sponsored the Consultation on Christian
Civility in New York City. This event addressed
both the current problem of the lack of civility
among American evangelicals and some of the issues out of which much recent incivility has flowed.
Twenty-five individuals participated directly in the
consultation, and many others have contributed to
this material since the conclusion of the event. In
January of 2018, another major resource was published, and insights from that resource have also
been incorporated into what follows. That resource
is *Still Evangelical? Insiders Reconsider Political, Social, and Theological Meaning*, edited by Mark Lab-
berton (Downers Grove, IL: InterVarsity 2018). The
WRF document is reprinted below, with permission.

While the World Reformed Fellowship remains vigorously committed to specifically REFORMED theology, we
also see ourselves as participating actively in the life of the
global evangelical church, a fact demonstrated by our organi-
zational membership in the World Evangelical Alliance. We
believe that the matters below are relevant both to the worldwide evangelical Christian community and to the specifically
Reformed part of that community. Thus, when we speak of

"evangelicals" and "evangelicalism," we have in view both Reformed evangelicals and those evangelicals who would not specifically self-identify as Reformed.

This document has been prepared in the form of "Affirmations," "Laments and Confessions," and "Commitments," and, at the end, areas which we believe need special emphasis are listed.

We affirm that we are and continue to be evangelicals as that term has been historically defined.

We lament that many of us have failed to speak and live the fullness of the gospel—the *euangelion*, from which the term "evangelical" is derived. **We confess** that this failure has dishonored the name of the One whose life, death, and resurrection are at the heart of that gospel. And **we commit** that, in both this small project and in all our words and deeds, we will energetically seek to embody the Lordship of Christ over all our thoughts, words, and actions.

We affirm that the *euangelion*, from which we take our name, has historically been and should always be focused on the *full* ministry and teaching of the Lord Jesus Christ.

We lament that, too often, we have narrowed our understanding of the gospel. **We confess** that we have allowed that narrowing to shape inappropriately both how we speak and how we act. And **we commit** that, going forward, we will intentionally focus our energies on embodying those areas of the gospel that each of us has individually neglected.

We affirm that the gospel involves unambiguous proclamation of at least the following theological truths: the full authority of the Old and New Testaments;

the necessity for saving and personal faith in the Lord Jesus Christ; the sovereignty of our Creator and Redeemer over all creation; and the requirement that everyone calling themselves Christians seek, in the power of the Holy Spirit, to live in obedience to *all* the commands of Scripture.

We lament that, we have frequently reduced Christian faith to mere intellectual assent. **We confess** that this is as much a violation of the essence of the gospel as any variation in our core doctrinal affirmations. And **we commit** that we will stand just as vigorously for *orthopraxy* as we have historically stood for *orthodoxy*.

We affirm that one central expression of the gospel is found in John 3: 16. However, we lament that we have not always emphasized fully and clearly enough that, for example, Matthew 25: 31–46—with Jesus' call to care for "the least of these"—is an equally central expression of the gospel. **We confess** that we have thus dishonored the One who is quoted in this passage. **We commit** that *both* central expressions will be on our lips and in our lives.

We affirm that all the Ten Commandments remain equally authoritative for Christians today, not because obeying them earns us a specific standing before God but because obeying them brings appropriate honor to the One who gave them.

We lament that we have often prioritized these commandments, focusing primarily on observable public behavior. **We confess** that doing so minimizes the seriousness of *all* violations of *any* of the commandments. And **we commit** that we will, in our teaching and in our lives, seek to honor God by emphasizing and being equally obedient to *all* his commands.

In light of the above, **we commit** ourselves to the following special emphases in these days:

1. There is only one Name to which we must look for our salvation, the Name of Jesus Christ. "In Christ alone" may hope be found.

2. One necessary and legitimate purpose and goal of the Christian life is "being bound for the promised land" of heaven.

3. An equally necessary and legitimate purpose and goal of the Christian life is "to make His blessings flow far as the curse is found."

4. *All* men and women are created in the image of God and must be treated accordingly. Christians must ensure that *all* members of *any* group that has been for any reason the objects of discrimination *know* that we, both in our words and in our lives, renounce and repent of such discrimination and seek to make sure that it is fully eliminated from our lives and our churches.

5. Beyond non-discrimination, Jesus has commanded us to love our neighbors—*all* our neighbors—and he has made it clear, specifically in the Parable of the Good Samaritan (Luke 10) that often the neighbor we should be active in loving is precisely the one who is very different from us.

6. Because the Bible places special emphasis on care for the poor and the oppressed, Christians must do the same. God's priorities (see Isaiah 58:1–12) must be our priorities.

7. While we must confront sin when we see it, the sin that we must be most diligent in confronting is that within our own hearts. (In the words of Jonathan Edwards, "Though Christian fortitude appears in withstanding and counteracting enemies without us; yet it much more appears in resisting and suppressing the enemies that are within us; *because they are our worst and strongest enemies and have greatest advantage against us*.")

8. We must remember in-fighting among Christians has often led to tragedy for the church's witness in the world. We must be gracious and civil in all our dealings with other Christians, *especially those brothers and sisters with whom we disagree*.

9. We must remember that the foundational documents of many Christian traditions interpret the Ninth commandment to mean that we must always "seek to promote the good name of our neighbor." Therefore, we must avoid inappropriate negative labeling of our theological opponents even as we seek to express our legitimate disagreements with them. As Jesus said, "By this everyone will know that you are my disciples, if you love one another" (John 13:35).

Document 2:
Social Media Policy of City Church of Houston, Texas

POSTING GUIDELINES:

- No posts should undermine the motto: Love the city to life.

- City Church's social media presence will be an accurate reflection of the church environment, vision and values. In an effort to maintain authenticity and establish real connections with fans and followers, posts will not downplay weaknesses or overplay strengths.

- Posts will avoid using insider-only language, terminology and phrases that may be unknown to many without discounting a gospel-oriented focus.

- Posts will appeal to secular, educated professionals and artists. Filter things through the lens of what they will think. Ensure our words are lovingly and respectfully engaging them rather than reinforcing their stereotypes of evangelicals and shaping City Church into a Christian subculture.

- Posts will be careful to avoid words or tones that are critical of civic and political leaders and may identify City Church in any way with a political party, personality or socio-political cause. We will tenaciously guard City Church as an "apolitical" space that exists to promote the centrality of Christ— keeping the main thing the main thing—and avoid anything that may possibly detract from this.

- Avoid posts that are critical of other Christian traditions, striving to be generous of others who identify as Christians.

- Because we want people to discover the freedom of grace, we will avoid statements that motivate by guilt or shame. Anything that hints of legalism is to be avoided.

- Avoid gender stereotypes and use gender inclusive language wherever possible (humankind rather than mankind), and use feminine pronouns at least as frequently as masculine, particularly when referring to professionals and artists.

- Posts will embrace a multiracial and multicultural voice.

HASHTAGS

Before choosing an event hashtag, check the current traffic within the selection on social media platforms, and confirm it is not already in use for another purpose.

AFILIATED PAGES

Any church ministry seeking to create an individual social media presence must seek approval from the Lead Pastor or Executive Director before the creation of the accounts. If additional social media pages obtain approval from church leadership, login and password information must be shared with City Church's social media manager in the event immediate access is needed.

NEGATIVE CONTENT

If a social media user posts negative content to a church account, the Lead Pastor will be notified to write a response on behalf of City Church. As a church that takes questions of unbelief seriously, the response will not attack the commenter, but seek to humbly engage the user in discussion. Often, negative-commenters don't think they will get a response, and when they do, they usually delete their own comment.

- Don't delete the comment.
- Respond promptly.
- Be respectful.

CRISIS RESPONSE

In the event of a church crisis, the Lead Pastor or Executive Director are the only authorized spokespersons on all social media accounts. They may direct others to post specific details, but all authorization begins with them.

STAFF GUIDELINES

City Church staff members are encouraged to be active on personal social media accounts. This allows staff members to tangibly uphold the church's vision and values by engaging the city of Houston through public social media posts that are outward facing in all things while displaying transparent love and celebrating the arts as a recovery of beauty.

Since City Church is committed to maintaining a gospel atmosphere, personal social media accounts should not be used to disperse sensitive or confidential church information, and staff members should refrain from publicizing political affiliations or polarizing opinions about controversial topics.

POLICY REVIEW

City Church's social media policy should be reviewed frequently to confirm the information is up-to-date, its online voice is still relevant and protocol is being followed or amended.

SELECTED BIBLE PASSAGES ABOUT THE POWER OF GOD'S WORD

Passages that show how God's Word sustains the human spirit:

> Save me, O God, by your name;
>   vindicate me by your might.
> Hear my prayer, O God;
>   listen to the words of my mouth.
> Arrogant foes are attacking me;
>   ruthless people are trying to kill me—
>   people without regard for God.
> Surely God is my help;
>   the Lord is the one who sustains me. (Psalm 54:1–4)

This is what the LORD says: "When seventy years are completed for Babylon, I will come to you and fulfill my good promise to bring you back to this place. For I know the plans I have for you," declares the Lord, "plans to prosper you and not to harm you, plans to give you hope and a future. Then you will call on me and come and pray to me, and I will listen to you. You will seek me and find me. When you seek me with all your heart, I will be found by you," declares the LORD, "and will bring you back from captivity. I will gather you from all the nations and places where I have banished you," declares the LORD, "and will bring you back to the place from which I carried you into exile." (Jeremiah 29:10–14)

Your statutes are my delight;
　　they are my counselors. (Psalm 119:24)

My comfort in my suffering is this:
　　Your promise preserves my life. (Psalm 119:50)

The law from your mouth is more precious to me
　　than thousands of pieces of silver and gold. (Psalm 119:72)

My soul faints with longing for your salvation,
　　but I have put my hope in your word. (Psalm 119:81)

Jesus returned to Galilee in the power of the Spirit, and news about him spread through the whole countryside. He was teaching in their synagogues, and everyone praised him.

He went to Nazareth, where he had been brought up, and on the Sabbath day he went into the synagogue, as was his custom. He stood up to read, and the scroll of the prophet Isaiah was handed to him. Unrolling it, he found the place where it is written:
　　"The Spirit of the Lord is on me,
　　　　because he has anointed me
　　　　to proclaim good news to the poor.
　　He has sent me to proclaim freedom for the prisoners
　　　　and recovery of sight for the blind,
　　to set the oppressed free,
　　　　to proclaim the year of the Lord's favor."

Then he rolled up the scroll, gave it back to the attendant and sat down. The eyes of everyone in the synagogue were fastened on him. He began by saying to them, "Today this scripture is fulfilled in your hearing." (Luke 4:14–21)

When evening came, his disciples went down to the lake, where they got into a boat and set off across the lake for Capernaum. By now it was dark, and Jesus had not yet joined them. A strong wind was blowing and the waters grew rough. When they had rowed about three or four miles, they saw Jesus approaching the boat, walking on the water; and they were frightened. But he said to them, "It is I; don't be afraid." (John 6:16–20)

"If you love me, keep my commands. And I will ask the Father, and he will give you another advocate to help you and be with you forever—the Spirit of truth. The world cannot accept him, because it neither sees him nor knows him. But you know him, for he lives with you and will be in you. I will not leave you as orphans; I will come to you. Before long, the world will not see me anymore, but you will see me. Because I live, you also will live." (John 14:15–19)

Then Jesus came to them and said, "All authority in heaven and on earth has been given to me. Therefore go and make disciples of all nations, baptizing them in the name of the Father and of the Son and of the Holy Spirit, and teaching them to obey everything I have commanded you. And surely I am with you always, to the very end of the age." (Matthew 28:18–20)

Dear friends, do not be surprised at the fiery ordeal that has come on you to test you, as though something strange were happening to you. But rejoice inasmuch as you participate in the sufferings of Christ, so that you may be overjoyed when his glory is revealed. If you are insulted because of the name of Christ, you are blessed, for the Spirit of glory and of God rests on you. (1 Peter 4:12–14)

Passages that show the power of God's word to judge and redeem:

"Woe to you, teachers of the law and Pharisees, you hypocrites! You shut the door of the kingdom of heaven in people's faces. You yourselves do not enter, nor will you let those enter who are trying to.

"Woe to you, teachers of the law and Pharisees, you hypocrites! You travel over land and sea to win a single convert, and when you have succeeded, you make them twice as much a child of hell as you are." (Matthew 23:13–15)

Jesus stepped into a boat, crossed over and came to his own town. Some men brought to him a paralyzed man, lying on a mat. When Jesus saw their faith, he said to the man, "Take heart, son; your sins are forgiven."

At this, some of the teachers of the law said to themselves, "This fellow is blaspheming!"

Knowing their thoughts, Jesus said, "Why do you entertain evil thoughts in your hearts? Which is easier: to say, 'Your sins are forgiven,' or to say, 'Get up and walk'? But I want you to know that the Son of Man has authority on earth to forgive sins." So he said to the paralyzed man, "Get up, take your mat and go home." Then the man got up and went home. When the crowd saw this, they were filled with awe; and they praised God, who had given such authority to man. (Matthew 9:1–8)

ENDNOTES

INTRODUCTION

1. David O'Reilly, "Controversial Theologian," *Philadelphia Inquirer*, July 26, 2008, https://www.philly.com/philly/news/homepage/20080726_Controversial_theologian.html.

2. Richard Mouw, *Uncommon Decency: Christian Civility in an Uncivil World* (Downers Grove, IL: InterVarsity, 1992, 2010).

CHAPTER 1

1. Scott Sauls, Instagram, https://www.instagram.com/p/Bt3egevh2AS/?utm_source=ig_share_sheet&igshid=yn5wh6nx19u0

2. John Calvin, *Commentaries on the Epistle of Paul to the Hebrews* (Grand Rapids: Baker Book House, 1998), p. 37.

3. Jean-Paul Sartre, *Nausea*, trans. Lloyd Alexander (New York: Spark Publishing, 2007), loc. 3234, Kindle.

4. Some evangelical scholars, most notably Nicolas Malebranche and Jonathan Edwards, responding to much earlier "Sartre-esque" philosophers, have suggested that our physical world

continues to exist only because God continues to create it anew by his powerful word at every moment. This perspective, called *occasionalism*, probably pushes the argument too far but it does raise for open-minded philosophers and theologians the question of why our world continues to exist as it has existed. Sartre powerfully points out that this need not be the case and, therefore, there must be some explanation of "the continuity of creation." What is that explanation if it is not the word of the Lord?

5. Martin Luther, "A Mighty Fortress Is Our God," trans. Frederick H. Hedge, https://www.hymnal.net/en/hymn/h/886.

6. Fleming Rutledge, *The Crucifixion: Understanding the Death of Jesus Christ* (Grand Rapids: Eerdmans, 2015), loc. 16281–16298, Kindle.

7. J. I. Packer, "Reflected Glory," *Christianity Today*, December 2003, 56.

8. Sinclair Ferguson, *The Christian Life: A Doctrinal Introduction* (Edinburgh: Banner of Truth, 1989), 11.

9. For a full discussion of what I have called the "power potential" of human language, see Kevin Vanhoozer, "From Speech Acts to Scripture Acts," Academia, 2001, https://www.academia.edu/1328484/From_Speech_Acts_to_Scripture_Acts.

10. Jim Elliott, *The Journals of Jim Elliott*, ed. Elizabeth Elliott, the Archives of Wheaton College, https://www2.wheaton.edu/bgc/archives/faq/20.htm.

11. Peter Jackson, dir., *The Lord of the Rings: The Return of the King* (Los Angeles: New Line Cinema, 2003).

12. Rachael Denhollander, reported in "Read Rachael Denhollander's Full Victim Impact Statement about Larry Nassar," CNN online, January 30, 2018, https://www.cnn.com/2018/01/24/us/rachael-denhollander-full-statement/index.html.

13. For example, Diane Langberg, *Suffering and the Heart of God* (Greensboro, NC: New Growth Press, 2015).

14. Diane Langberg, "A Missional Response to Global Violence against Women," in *Reformed Means Missional: Following Jesus into the World*, ed. Samuel T. Logan, Jr. (Greensboro, NC: New Growth Press, 2013) 130.

15. Diane Langberg, "Trauma as Mission Field," World Reformed Fellowship, June 5, 2011, http://wrfnet.org/resources/2011/06/trauma-mission-field-wrf-board-member-dr-diane-langberg.

CHAPTER 2

1. Amanda Hess, "Battle Cry," *The New York Times Magazine*, August 20, 2017, 10. Emphasis added.

2. This modern English version of the catechism is written by John Barrs and used with his permission. Accessed from the website of the International Presbyterian Church West Liss, *The Westminster Larger Catechism*, www.ipc-liss.com/userfiles/file/wc_1_cat.doc.

3. *The Heidelberg Catechism*, website of the Center for Reformed Theology and Apologetics, http://www.reformed.org/documents/heidelberg.html.

4. The thirteen Bible passages cited by both catechisms are Proverbs 12:22; Proverbs 13:5, Proverbs 19:5, Psalm 15:3, Psalm 50:19, Psalm 50:20, Romans 1:29–30, Matthew 7:1–2, Luke 6:37, John 8:44, 1 Corinthians 13:6, Ephesians 4:25, and 1 Peter 4:8.

5. *The Baltimore Catechism*, questions 265–268, CatholiCity, https://www.catholicity.com/baltimore-catechism/lesson20.html.

6. *Catechism of the Methodist Episcopal Church* (New York: Carlton & Phillips, 1855), 64, https://books.google.com/books?id=6QIyAQAAMAAJ.

7. *The Baptist Catechism*, Credo Covenant, https://credocovenant.com/2013/11/11/the-baptist-catechism/.

8. *The Catechism of St. Philaret*, Provoslavieto.com, http://www.pravoslavieto.com/docs/eng/Orthodox_Catechism_of_Philaret.htm.

9. John Calvin, *Commentaries on the Last Four Books of Moses, Arranged in the Form of a Harmony* (Grand Rapids: Baker, 1998), 3:179–80.

10. Ernst Cassirer, *Language and Myth* (New York: Harper and Brothers, 1946), loc. 95, Kindle. See also Bland Branshard's review of Cassirer's *An Essay on Man* in *The Philosophical Review* 54, no. 5 (September 1945): 509–10, republished at AnthonyFlood.com, http://www.anthonyflood.com/blanshardcassireressayonman.htm.

11. Andrew Davids, "The Power of a Name: The Power of Naming," My Jewish Learning, accessed February 13, 2019, https://www.myjewishlearning.com/article/the-power-of-a-name-the-power-of-naming/.

12. John Calvin, *Commentary on The Acts of the Apostles* (Grand Rapids: Baker, 1998), 1:472.

13. Frank Viola, "Warning: The World Is Watching How We Christians Treat One Another," The Deeper Journey, October 25, 2016, https://www.patheos.com/blogs/frankviola/warning/.

14. James Davidson Hunter, *To Change the World: The Irony, Tragedy, and Possibility of Christianity in the Late Modern World* (New York: Oxford University Press, 2010), loc. 4875, Kindle.

15. Jonathan Edwards, *Works of Jonathan Edwards Online*, *Volume 2: A Treatise Concerning Religious Affections* (New Haven, CT: Jonathan Edwards Center at Yale University, 2008), 350.

CHAPTER 3

1. Stuart Dauermann, "Sympathy for Esau and The Arab/Israel Conflict," *The Messianic Agenda*, November 19, 2012.

2. Bill Thayer, "Ammianus Marcellinus," http://penelope.uchicago.edu/Thayer/E/Roman/Texts/Ammian/Introduction*.html

3. Ammianus Marcellinus, *Res Gestae*, trans. J. C. Rolfe, Loeb Classical Library, 1935–40, 22:5:3–4, http://skookumpete.com/books/ResGestae.htm.

4. Mark Galli and Ted Olsen, ed., *131 Christians Everyone Should Know* (Nashville, TN: Holman, 2000), 17.

5. Socrates Scholasticus, "The Death of Arius," chap. 38 in *Nicene and Post-Nicene Fathers, Series 2, Volume 2: Socrates and Sozomenus Ecclesiastical Histories*, comp. Philip Schaff, Christian Classics Ethereal Library, http://www.ccel.org/ccel/schaff/npnf202.ii.iv.xxxviii.html.

6. Rod Dreher, *The Benedict Option: A Strategy for Christians in a Post-Christian Nation* (New York: Penguin Random House, 2017), 22.

7. John B. Payne, "Zwingli and Luther: The Giant vs. Hercules," *Christian History*, 1984, http://www.christianitytoday.com/history/issues/issue-4/zwingli-and-luther-giant-vs-hercules.html.

8. Roland Bainton, *Here I Stand: A Life of Martin Luther* (New York: Abingdon Press, 1950), 318–20.

9. Bainton, *Here I Stand*, 270–71.

10. Martin Luther, "Against the Robbing and Murdering Hordes of Peasants," http://zimmer.csufresno.edu/~mariterel/against_the_robbing_and_murderin.htm.

11. *Encyclopedia Britannica Online*, s.v. "Peasants' War," accessed February 14, 2019, https://www.britannica.com/event/Peasants-War.

12. David Edwards, *Christian England: From the Reformation to the 18th Century* (Grand Rapids: Eerdmans, 1983), 22, 82, 137.

13. The tract is "A Brief Discourse Against the Outward Apparel and Ministering Garments of the Popish Church: The Unfolding of the Pope's Attire," quoted by W. H. Stowell in *History of the Puritans in England Under the Reigns of the Tudors and the Stuarts* (New York: Carter and Brothers, 1849), 142–43.

14. M. M. Knappen, *Tudor Puritanism: A Chapter in the History of Idealism* (Chicago: University of Chicago Press, 1939), 190–91.

15. Bancroft's writings against the Puritans are contained in his work, *Dangerous Positions and Proceedings: Published and Practised Within This Iland of Brytaine, Under Pretence of Reformation, and for the Presbiteriall Discipline*. See also *Encyclopedia Britannica Online*, s.v. "Richard Bancroft," accessed February 14, 2019, https://www.britannica.com/biography/Richard-Bancroft.

16. Margo Todd, in her review of *Richard Bancroft and Elizabethan Anti-Puritanism* by Patrick Collinson, *The American Historical Review* 119, no. 4 (October 2014): 1349–50, https://academic.oup.com/ahr/article/119/4/1349/44403.

17. Christopher Hill, *The World Turned Upside Down: Radical Ideas During the English Revolution* (New York: Viking Penguin, 1975), 13–18.

18. David Edwards, *A Concise History of English Christianity From Roman Britain to the Present Day* (London: HarperCollins, 1998), 78–81.

19. Alan Heimert, *Religion and the American Mind: From the Great Awakening to the Revolution* (Cambridge, MA: Harvard University Press, 1966), see especially chapter 10, "The People, the Best Governors."

20. John Adams, "Letter to Hezekiah Niles on the American Revolution, 13 February, 1818," National Humanities Center Resource Toolbox, http://nationalhumanitiescenter.org/ows/seminars/revolution/Adams-Niles.pdf.

21. Charles Chauncy, *Seasonable Thoughts on the State of Religion in New England*, Evans Early American Imprint Collection, 1:324–325, https://quod.lib.umich.edu/e/evans/N04182.0001.001/1:6?rgn =div1;view=fulltext.

22. Chauncy, *Seasonable Thoughts*.

23. Gilbert Tennent, "The Danger of an Unconverted Ministry," CBN, http://www1.cbn.com/danger-unconverted-ministry.

24. Ibid.

25. Jonathan Edwards, "Some Thoughts Concerning the Present Revival of Religion in New England and the Way in Which It Ought to Be Acknowledged and Promoted" in *The Works of Jonathan Edwards* (Edinburgh: Banner of Truth, 1974), 1:415.

26. Edwards, "Some Thoughts," 415–16.

27. Jonathan Edwards, *A Treatise Concerning Religious Affections* (New Haven, CT: Yale University Press, 1959), 345.

28. Ibid.

29. Ibid., 352.

30. William S. Barker and Samuel T. Logan, Jr., Eds., *Sermons That Shaped America: Reformed Preaching from 1630 to 2001* (Phillipsburg, NJ: Presbyterian and Reformed, 2003), 123.

31. George Marsden, *Jonathan Edwards: A Life* (New Haven, CT: Yale University Press, 2003), 293.

32. Ibid.

33. Ibid.

34. "The Christianity Today Board of Directors Honors Our Founder, Billy Graham," *Christianity Today*, April 2018, 9.

35. Albert Mohler, "Heresy and Humility—Lessons from the Current Controversy," June 28, 2016, https://albertmohler.com/2016/06/28/heresy/.

36. Scotty Smith, "When Sharp and Serious Disagreements Threaten," website of The Gospel Coalition, October 7, 2018, https://www.thegospelcoalition.org/blogs/scotty-smith/sharp-serious-disagreements-threaten/.

CHAPTER 4

1. The Orthodox Presbyterian Church, *Report of the Committee to Study Republication*, 2016, https://www.opc.org/GA/republication.html.

2. Gerard Baker on *Meet the Press*. Aired January 1, 2017, on NBC. https://www.nbcnews.com/meet-the-press/meet-press-1-1-17-n702006.

3. Joel Stein, "How Trolls Are Ruining the Internet," *Time*, August 18, 2016, http://time.com/magazine/us/4457098/august-29th-2016-vol-188-no-8-u-s/.

4. Tim Challies, "The Duties Required by the Ninth Commandment in a Social Media World," *@Challies*, Spetember, 26, 2018, https://www.challies.com/articles/the-decline-of-the-ninth-commandment-in-the-rise-of-social-media/.

5. Ligon Duncan, "A Ten Point Social Media Strategy," reported by Justin Taylor, website of The Gospel Coalition, October 2, 2018, https://www.thegospelcoalition.org/blogs/justin-taylor/10-point-social-media-strategy/.

6. Archbishop Foley Beach: "A Christian Code of Ethics for Using Social Media." https://prydain.wordpress.com/2019/03/14/abp-foley-beach-a-christian-code-of-ethics-for-using-social-media/. Used with permission.

7. See Matt Dickinson, "Research Finds Bullying Link to Child Suicides," website of the *Independent*, June 13, 2010, http://www. independent.co.uk/news/uk/home-news/research-finds-bullying-link-to-child-suicides-1999349.html.

8. "What Is Cyberbullying," The U.S. Department of Health and Human Services website, stopbullying.gov, February 7, 2018, https://www.stopbullying.gov/cyberbullying/what-is-it/index. html.

9. Bernard Bailyn, *The Ideological Origins of the American Revolution* (Cambridge, MA, Harvard University Press, 1967. See especially chapter 6, "The Contagion of Liberty." If you read Bailyn's book together with Mark Noll's magnificent, *Princeton and the Republic, 1768–1822: The Search for Christian Enlightenment in the Era of Samuel Stanhope Smith* (Princeton, NJ: Princeton University Press, 1989), you will get a very clear sense of how "the contagion of liberty" swept through the American church at the end of the eighteenth century.

10. Bailyn, *Ideological Origins*, 230–319.

11. See my discussion of this topic in "Academic Freedom at Christian Institutions," *Christian Scholar's Review* 21, no. 2 (December 1991): 169–74.

12. John Calvin, *Institutes of the Christian Religion,* ed. John T. McNeill, trans. Ford Lewis Battles (Philadelphia: Westminster Press, 1960), 2:1014.

13. Greg Gilbert, "Is There Such a Thing as Church Authority?," 9Marks, September 30, 2016, https://www.9marks.org/article/is-there-such-a-thing-as-church-authority/.

CHAPTER 5

1. For example, when Isaiah described the "suffering servant" in chapter 53 of his prophecy, did he fully understand that the servant would be God incarnate? For more information on this

subject, see the explanation provided by Dr. William Evans at https://theecclesialcalvinist.wordpress.com/tag/christotelic-interpretation/.

2. See Mouw, *Uncommon Decency*, 90.

3. Jonathan Edwards, *A Careful and Strict Inquiry into the Modern Prevailing Notions of That Freedom of Will Which Is Supposed to Be Essential to Moral Agency, Virtue and Vice, Reward and Punishment, Praise and Blame*, in *The Works of Jonathan Edwards*, ed. Paul Ramsey (New Haven, CT: Yale University Press, 2009), 1:374.

4. After I completed this manuscript, The *Philadelphia Inquirer* published an editorial which also makes suggestions about how to talk to and about those with whom we disagree. Although this material does not specifically address Christian responsibilities, it does provide suggestions similar to those in this chapter. See Carolyn Hax, "On Surviving Political Talk," *The Philadelphia Inquirer,* July 4, 2018, C5.

5. See Mouw's excellent points here, *Uncommon Decency*, 50ff.

6. Joni Eareckson Tada, *Life in the Balance: Biblical Answers for the Issues of Our Day* (Ventura, CA: Regal, 2010).

7. The Religious Coalition for Reproductive Choice, http://rcrc.org/.

8. Alan Noble, Michael Wear, Vincent Bacote, Justin Giboney, Art Hooker, Joel Hunter, Skye Jethani, Janet Vestal Kelly, Shapri D. Lomaglio, Gabe Lyons, Richard Mouw, Gabriel Salguero, Jemar Tisby, Autumn Hanna Vandehei, and Tish Harrison Warren, "Public Faith: A Christin Voice for the Common Good," http://www.publicfaith.us/.

9. Matt Chandler, "Abortion is Everyone's Issue," website of The Village Church, January 26, 2006, https://www.tvcresources.net/resource-library/articles/abortion-is-everyones-issue.

10. Pope Francis, "Gaudete et Exultate: On the Call to Holiness in Today's World," website of the Holy See, March 19, 2018, 101, http://w2.vatican.va/content/francesco/en/apost_exhortations/documents/

papa-francesco_esortazione-ap_20180319_gaudete-et-exsultate.
html.

11. See, for example, Kallie Kohl's blog post, "Words Are Not
Enough," *Center Insights* (blog), *Care-Net*, October 31, 2016, https://
www.care-net.org/center-insights-blog/words-are-not-enough.

12. Matthew Parris, "Abortion Triumphalism Is Deeply Troubling,"
The Times: Scotland, June 2, 2018, 21.

13. Francis Schaeffer, *How Should We Then Live: The Rise and Fall
of Western Thought and* Culture (Wheaton, IL: Crossway, 2005).

14. Richard Mouw's discussion of motives is especially helpful. See
Uncommon Decency, 144ff.

15. See, for example, Daniel Wells, "Seven Days That Divide the
World—Apologist John Lennox Interacts with 6/24 Creationists,"
The Aquila Report, January 5, 2012, https://www.theaquilareport.
com/seven-days-that-divide-the-world-apologist-john-lennox-
interacts-with-624-creationists/.

16. See, for example, Tim Bayly, "Report of the PCA Study
Committee on Women in the Church (1): Kathy Keller 'Voting
Member,'" *BaylyBlog*, April 21, 2017, http://baylyblog.com/
blog/2017/04/report-pca-study-committee-women-church-1-
kathy-keller-voting-member.

17. See, for example, Emma Green, "A Conservative Christian
Battle Over Gender," *The Atlantic*, July 5, 2017, https://www.
theatlantic.com/politics/archive/2017/07/truths-table-gender-
race/532407/.

18. Dan Brown, *The Da Vinci Code* (New York: Doubleday,
2003), 252.

19. See C. Ramsey Fahs, "In Historic Move, Harvard to Penalize
Final Clubs, Greek Organizations," *The Harvard Crimson*, May
8, 2016, http://www.thecrimson.com/article/2016/5/6/college-
sanctions-clubs-greeklife/.

20. Philip Payne, *Man and Woman: One in Christ* (Grand Rapids: Zondervan, 2009) and Carrie Sandom, *Different by Design: God's Blueprint for Men and Women* (Tain, Ross-shire, Scotland: Christian Focus, 2014).

21. *Christianity Today* editors, "John MacArthur's 'Statement on Social Justice' Is Aggravating Evangelicals: Christians Are Talking Past Each Other Once Again. What's Going On?" in *Christianity Today*, September 12, 2018, https://www.christianitytoday.com/ct/2018/september-web-only/john-macarthur-statement-social-justice-gospel-thabiti.html.

22. *Agenda for Synod 2016: Responding to God's Gracious Call* (Grand Rapids, MI: The Christian Reformed Church in North America, 2016), 402.

23. Jonathan Edwards, "The Great Christian Doctrine of Original Sin Defended," Jonathan Edwards Center at Yale University, *Original Sin (WJE Online Vol. 3)*, 140, http://edwards.yale.edu

24. Ibid., 132.

25. Specific suggestions relating primarily to how evangelical Christian colleges should treat LBGT students are made by Alan Noble, "Keeping Faith Without Hurting LGBT Students," *The Atlantic*, August 15, 2016, https://www.theatlantic.com/politics/archive/2016/08/christian-colleges-lgbt/495815/.

26. Wesley Hill, *Washed and Waiting: Reflections on Christian Faithfulness and Homosexuality* (Grand Rapids: Zondervan, 2010).

27. Scott Sauls, "Can Christians and the LGTBQ Community be Friends?" *Q*, September 7, 2016, http://qideas.org/articles/can-christians-and-the-lgbtq-community-be-friends/.

28. Andy Crouch, "It's Time to Reckon with Celebrity Power," website of The Gospel Coalition, March 24, 2018, https://www.thegospelcoalition.org/article/time-reckon-celebrity-power/.